# PHEZU

## Practical · Handy · Easy · Zulu

*A beginner's course*
*by*

**J. B. TOWNSHEND**

<Shuter & Shooter

Shuter & Shooter

PIETERMARITZBURG • CAPE TOWN • RANDBURG

Shuter & Shooter (Pty) Ltd
Gray's Inn, 230 Church Street
Pietermaritzburg, South Africa 3201

First edition 1990 (ISBN 0 7960 0220 7)
Second edition (ISBN 0 7960 0387 4)
Third edition 1993
*Third impression 1996*

ISBN 0 7960 0569 9

Set in 10 on 12 pt Times Roman
Printed by The Natal Witness
Printing and Publishing Company (Pty) Ltd
Pietermaritzburg
8997LH

# *Preface*

Many adults express a desire or have made an attempt to learn to speak Zulu, and it is to assist such people that PRACTICAL HANDY EASY ZULU (PHEZULU) has been published. The author has been teaching Zulu to adult beginners intermittently over the last 16 years and his experience in this field has prompted him to produce this work.

This represents the manualised version of the notes the author uses in his Beginners' course and retains much of the teacher-student relationship in the language used and explanations offered — some of them quite novel. It has some unusual features, such as the inclusion in the Contents of the type of sentence dealt with in each section (which the subject heading alone might not adequately convey) and the occasional reference to the differences between Zulu and Fanakalo. The English-Zulu vocabulary at the end of the manual also contains phrases and expressions which will assist in conversation in addition to all the words used in the Course (with their appropriate references).

The tapes are a vital ingredient of this course. Unless the services of a Zulu-speaker are available, it would otherwise be difficult to master the pronunciations and obtain confidence in the 'flow' of spoken Zulu which the tapes provide.

The PHEZULU manual is aimed at the adult person who has no prior knowledge of Zulu and is learning on his own. No attempt has been made to present this manual as a textbook of Zulu grammar (reference to a few such books is made in the Acknowledgements). The learning of any language, however, involves a grasp of certain grammatical rules. In this Course, where a point of grammar is essential to understanding the structures involved, it is given in the simplest language possible. Similarly, where there are alternative ways of expressing an idea, the easiest has been chosen. Simplicity, with correctness, is the keynote.

The Course also contains a brief reference to some of the more important aspects of Zulu culture, since a knowledge of these is important in achieving a better mutual understanding.

The duration of the live course, allowing for revision, questions and practice in class, is 60 hours. The student working on his own should thus be able to master this Course within a period of 3 to 4 months.

The Zulu word from which the title of this manual is taken is PHEZULU (the H being not pronounced). It means: Above, On Top and it is the author's sincere hope that those who use this manual will indeed be able to surmount the difficulties that a new language poses, and, with its help, master this most interesting and rewarding language — isiZULU.

# *Acknowledgements*

The author acknowledges that in compiling the Phezulu manual, extensive
reference has been made to the following publications:
Learn Zulu and Learn More Zulu (S. Nyembezi)
Masikhulume isiZulu (Kotze & Klopper)
Sanibona I and II (B. Muller & B. Mthethwa)
Hhawu, Sesikhuluma isiZulu (Zulu for Primary Schools)
Siyafunda I and II (T V Series)
Zulu — English Dictionary (Doke & Vilakazi)

# Introduction

## A.   Some features of Zulu

It is one of the Nguni group of languages, related to Xhosa, SiSwati and Ndebele. The other main language group is Sotho, from which it differs greatly.

All words end in a vowel (a, e, i, o, u) and a word written or spoken as e.g. umfaan is incorrect — it should be umfana.

The accent is generally on the syllable before the last (penultimate) e.g. i*zin*to (things) -ha*mbi*le (has gone) u*ya*phi? (where are you going?) eMpa*ng*eni (at Empangeni). If a word is enlarged by the addition of a syllable (a common feature of Zulu) the accent is altered accordingly e.g. i*si*tsha (dish), isi*tsh*ana (a small dish), i*nta*ba (hill, mountain), enta*be*ni (on the hill/mountain).

The final syllable of a Zulu word is usually 'weak' (unaccentuated).

As with all languages, there has been a borrowing of foreign words. These relate mainly to things and ideas unknown in their culture and introduced by Whites. The main borrowings have been from English and Afrikaans. Examples: From English — imfologo (fork) from fork, ihhotela (hotel) from hotel, ushukela (sugar) from sugar, isheke (cheque) from cheque, galanta (guarantee) from guarantee.

From Afrikaans — idolobha (town) from dorp, umese (knife) from mes, itafula (table) from tafel, ibhulukwe (trousers) from broek, isonto (church, Sunday) from Sondag.

English has also adopted words from Zulu, with words such as donga (from udonga — a gully, wall), fundi (an expert, from fundisa — to teach), the zibi can (from izibi — rubbish) and most recently, indaba (from indaba, a matter to discuss).

### Relationship with Fanakalo

Many people speak to Blacks in Fanakalo and some are under the impression that they are speaking Zulu. Fanakalo has been a means of communication in southern Africa for about 100 years and probably had its origins in Zulu/Xhosa, adapted to meet the needs of communication between the various Black tribesmen, who came from all over southern Africa to work on the mines, and their White supervisors. From there it spread gradually to other spheres such as domestic service and industry. It contains many Zulu words and constructions, but one who speaks Fanakalo, although he may be communicating, is certainly not speaking Zulu. Fanakalo is becoming increasingly unacceptable to Zulu people, both because of its 'pidgin English' connotations and identification with the master-servant relationship. In any sphere other than the mining industry or where members of different tribes are employed in significant numbers, the use of Fanakalo is not conducive to good human relations. The author has had many speakers of Fanakalo wishing to learn Zulu and to assist such people to break away from the incorrect usages they have been used to, appropriate comments have been made in the relevant sections of the Course.

## B. Pronunciations

Zulu was not a written language and the first people to reduce it to writing were missionaries and explorers, who naturally employed our European alphabet. Some of the sounds of Zulu, however, cannot be catered for by our alphabet, and another unusual feature is the use of clicks (which were inherited from the Bushmen and Hottentot languages) of which there are three in Zulu.

Whereas in English some letters may have differing pronunciations, e.g. the letter 'a' in the words: man, may, mar, the Zulu pronunciations, which are itemised below, are generally constant

### Vowels ▶

A  as in 'far'  *Examples*: vala (shut)  lala (sleep)  umfana (boy)
E  as in 'wet'  *Examples*: geza (wash)  sebenza (work)  yebo (yes)
I  as in 'inn'  *Examples*: biza (call)  siza (help)  ngi (I, me)  fika (come)
O  as in 'ore'  (never as in 'hope' as often mistakenly pronounced by Whites)
　　　　　　　*Examples*: bona (see)  izolo (yesterday)  into (thing)
U  as in 'full'  *Examples*: vula (open)  funa (want)  umuntu (person)

### Clicks

C  The sound made as when expressing annoyance or sorrow. With jaws slightly open, place the tip of the tongue against the upper teeth, then pull the tongue smartly backwards.

*Examples:*
▷  cela (ask for)  iculo (song)
▷  kancane (a little)  cabanga (think)

Q  Made prominent in the Click Song. With jaws open, press the tongue against the roof of the mouth, then pull it sharply downwards.

*Examples:*
▷  qala (begin)  qeda (finish)  iqanda (egg)

X  As used when urging a horse when riding. With jaws slightly open, press the tongue against the top teeth, then pull air in from the right side of the mouth by sharply pulling the tongue away to the left.

*Examples:*
▷  xabana (quarrel)  xosha (chase)  xoxa (converse)

In some words, the click letters c, q and x may be preceded by n or g, but this does not affect the basic sound of the click in question.

### Other Consonants

The remaining letters of the alphabet are given the customary English sounds, but make special note of the following:

G  is always 'hard', as in 'got', never soft as in 'gin'.

*Examples:*
▷  gula (be ill)  ganga (be naughty). But see remarks under K below.

H  is normal, as in 'hand', e.g. hamba (go) but when it follows a consonant the effect is to expel air (which does not alter the basic sound of such consonant) i.e.

▷ BH — as in 'bed'

*Examples*:

bhala (write)  bhema (smoke)

▷ CH — never as in 'chew'

*Examples*:

cha (no)  chitha (waste)

▷ KH — as in 'calm'

*Examples*: ˙

khala (cry)  khipha (take out)

▷ HH (previously a single H, now re-introduced) A voiced H, followed by a vowel.

*Examples*:

ihhashi (horse)  hhayi (no!)  ihhovisi (office)

PH — as in 'pen' (never as in 'pheasant')

*Examples*:

▷  pheka (cook)  phinda (repeat)  pho (well then)

SH — this is exceptional in that it is pronounced exactly as in English, as in 'shut' without any effect of air being expelled.

*Examples*:

▷  shisa (be hot)  shesha (hurry)

▷ TH — as in 'tell' (never as in 'this')

*Examples*:

thatha (take)  thela (pour)

K  has the ordinary English sound.

*Examples*:

▷  kubi (it is bad)  ekuseni (early). In some words, however, it is nearer to a 'g' than a 'k', such as:

o  sika (cut) — pronounced as you would 'seagull' without the -ll

o  kahle (well) — pronounced almost as the 'g' in 'garter'

L  is a normal sound, but when it follows H or D, the effect is as follows:

HL  is like the Welsh LL (as in Llandudno)

*Examples*:

o  hlala (sit, stay) which sounds almost like 'shlala' except that there is no 's':

o  hlupha (worry, annoy) pronounced almost as 'shloopah' except that there is no 's'

DL  is pronounced as for HL (above) except that it is voiced and does not have the element of the 'sh'. It is pronounced as in 'pedlar'.

*Examples*:

▷  indlebe (ear)  dlala (play)  dla (eat)  indlovu (elephant)

**General note on pronunciations**

There are many other pronunciation variations but as they are not of fundamental importance to the beginner and could confuse, these variants are not discussed here.

If the help of a Zulu-speaker can be enlisted it would be an invaluable aid to correct pronunciation. All above pronunciations are, however, recorded on the cassette, as are most of the Zulu words used in this course.

## C. Grammatical terms

In learning any language it is not possible for the student to avoid all reference to grammar. This course having been designed for adults, many of whom may have left school years ago, and also to assist those whose mother-tongue is not English, a list of the grammatical terms used in the course, with easy-to-understand explanations, is set out below. Some terms are considered to be so well-known that their inclusion is not warranted (e.g. sentence, phrase, singular, plural etc.). In general, grammatical terms have been used only where an alternative word or expression is clumsy or does not adequately convey the meaning.

*Adjective*   describes something or someone e.g. your (possessive adjective), pretty (descriptive), two (numeral), only (quantitative), those (demonstrative)

*Adverb*   describes an action in respect of Place (e.g. outside), Time (e.g. early), Manner (e.g. nicely)

*Coalescence*   See *fusion* (below)

*Concord*   is the link between a subject and the action it governs (It is similar to a pronoun but there are important differences.)

*Conjunctions*   are words joining separate actions/words e.g. and, but, because

*Consonants*   are all the letters of the alphabet except the vowels (a, e, i, o and u)

*Demonstratives*   describe position in relation to the speaker e.g. this, that

*Fusion*   is the result of two vowels being merged into one to create a new sound

*Imperative*   is a Command

*Indefinite*   is the word 'it' when not describing a specific thing e.g. it is good, it's hot, or 'a/an' as distinct from 'the' e.g. a person, an event

*Infinitive*   is the word 'to' before a verb e.g. to go, to see. It must not be confused with the word 'to' denoting movement towards for which see *prepositions* (below)

*Inflexion*   is a change in the pitch or tone of a sound

*Interrogative*   is a Question

*Locative*   is the place where an action takes place e.g. at home, to school, in the water. In Zulu, *one* word acts to include the preposition (see below) and the noun where the action takes place

*Modification*   means making changes to

*Negative*   is the word 'not' e.g. I am not going, don't talk, he is not here

*Noun*   is a person, animal or thing e.g. Joe, man, dog, table

*Object*   is the person or thing that has the action done to him/it e.g. they see *you*, I want *water*, call *her*

*Possessive*   describes ownership e.g. my, your, our, their

*Prefix*   is something added to the beginning of a word

*Preposition*   indicates the place of an action e.g. to, from, in, at, on (in Zulu these are not separate words but are included in the Locative)

*Pronoun*   is a word which stands instead of a noun e.g. these (Demonstrative), all (Quantitative), himself (Absolute) but the English pronouns I, you, he, it etc. do not have a direct equivalent in Zulu (for which see *concord* above)

*Subject*   is the person or thing that does the action e.g. *John* is going, the *dog* is running, *babies* cry, *we* want food

*Suffix*   is something added to the end of a word

*Syllables*   are the units which make up a word, each having its own sound e.g.
    animal (3 syllables), father (2 syllables), he (1 syllable)

*Tense*   is the time an action takes place (Present, Past and Future)

*Verbs*   are words indicating action e.g. go, see, hear, take

*Vowels*   are the letters A, E, I, O and U

## D.   General notes

### 1.   Structure

This course has been designed to encourage communication with Zulu-speakers. The sounds may at first appear strange and the pronunciation difficult, but the student is urged to practise as early in the course, and as much, as possible. The course is structured to this end, commencing with the words relating to persons, followed by questions (so as to encourage the interplay of question and answer), then branches out into other essential topics. No topic has been given in-depth treatment, as the course is essentially introductory and elementary. A second manual providing greater coverage is under consideration.

### 2.   Practice

The usual reaction by the average Zulu person to being addressed in his own language is one of pleasure and he is usually only too willing to enter into a conversation and to correct mistakes. You will probably understand very little of what he is saying (the need to speak slowly is often not appreciated!) but do not let this deter you. Try and recognise words you know — you will probably understand more than you think. A few sentences to help in this connection are given in paragraph 18.

### 3.   Study guide and note re tapes

The suggested method of learning is to study a lesson and the examples quoted and to repeat the latter aloud once or twice. Thereafter do the exercises for that lesson, checking your work with the answers at the back. Then go through the chapter again, this time with the tape. The two tapes are an optional extra and if the services of a Zulu-speaker are available, they may not be required. Selected words, phrases and sentences appear on the tapes and coverage is greater in the first part of the Course, where the student needs greater exposure to pronunciations and Zulu methods of expression. They have been provided with the following objects:

(a)  To teach correct pronunciation.

(b)  To assist in self-correction of sentences and exercises.

(c)  To accustom the student to the sound of spoken Zulu.

(d)  To act as 'refresher' when revising without the manual e.g. in the car, kitchen, workshop, etc.

Items on the casette are marked in this Manual thus: ▶: entire section; ▷: entire line; ○: word or sentence. In the case of vocabulary, the Zulu word is spoken twice with an interval between them. Where sentences are involved, the

Zulu is spoken three times. The English sentence is followed by the Zulu equivalent, at a slow pace, then a pause, then repeated (also at a slow pace to allow the student time to absorb it or repeat it aloud), then finally repeated at a faster pace approximating what would be heard in a normal conversation. In many instances, and especially at the beginning of the course, the English sentence is given twice: firstly, as spoken in English, then re-phrased in the form in which it is said in Zulu. This has been done to assist the student to absorb the Zulu way of expression and to break down any tendency to translate literally from the English.

Where the translation is from Zulu into English, the Zulu is spoken at normal conversational speed, then repeated more slowly, then the English equivalent is given — in many cases, the English is given twice: first, literally, as given in the Zulu, and then in colloquial English.

The exercises set at the end of each lesson are not on the tape, because the examples set out in the lessons illustrating each construction, give sufficient exposure to the correct word order, pronunciation, etc.

## 4.  Vocabulary

The Vocabulary given at various stages of the course contains basic words relevant to simple conversations, but it is very limited in scope and it is recommended that a simple dictionary be acquired (preferably English — Zulu and Zulu — English). The Manual sets out basic structures only, with a few illustrations of each subject being dealt with: the student should thereafter make up his own sentences from the vocabulary given. Remember that the two essentials for success are learning a vocabulary and frequent practice.

## 5.  Additional Appendix

Advantage has been taken of the need for a second edition to add a new Appendix which appears as Appendix II on page 117. References are to items in the main body of the manual.

# Contents

For ease of reference, the type of sentence covered by each topic in this manual is quoted in the relevant paragraph in the Index below.

## APPENDIX I

## APPENDIX II

# CHAPTER ONE

Personal subjectival concords
Sentence formation
Incomplete actions
Questions
Replies

## 1  Parties involved in communicating

The main objective of this Course is to encourage the student to communicate in Zulu. In any conversation to or about people, the following six parties are involved and when used as the subject (i.e. performing the action) they are:
▷  Singular: I NGI-  You U-(low tone)  He/she U-(high tone)
▷  Plural: We SI-  You NI-  They BA-
They must be well learnt as they are in frequent use in this course. Although they perform similar functions as the English personal pronouns, they are not the same as pronouns (e.g. they cannot stand alone — see para 2(a) below) hence in this course they will be referred to as Concords, which is the grammatical term for this feature in Zulu.

## 2.  Sentence formation

Zulu sentences follow a similar word order to English, i.e. the person or thing that does the action (the subject), then the action (the verb) and thereafter any additional words such as an object, adverb, exclamation, etc.
Study the following sentences:
○  I see a person
Ngi- bona umuntu = Ngibona umuntu
○  You smoke a lot
U- bhema kakhulu = Ubhema kakhulu
○  He sees a dog
U- bona inja = Ubona inja
○  Joe works well
uJoe u- sebenza kahle = UJoe usebenza kahle
○  We want sugar

---

Key to Symbols in text to be used in conjunction with tapes:
  ○  The word or sentence
  ▷  The complete line
  ▶  The complete section

*1*

Si- funa ushukela = Sifuna ushukela
- We want some sugar
  Si- funa ushukela = Sifuna ushukela
- They work in Durban
  Ba- sebenza eThekwini = Basebenza eThekwini
- The people work in Durban
  Abantu ba- sebenza eThekwini = Abantu basebenza eThekwini
- I drink tea
  Ngi- phuza itiye = Ngiphuza itiye
- I am drinking tea
  Ngi- phuza itiye = Ngiphuza itiye
- We help children
  Si-siza abantwana = Sisiza abantwana
- We are helping children
  Si- siza abantwana = Sisiza abantwana

The following points emerge:

(a) The Concord cannot stand alone (as the English pronoun does). It must be incorporated into the action word (verb) and this is the reason it is shown followed by a hyphen (-)

(b) The Concord for You (u-) is the same as for He/She (u-) but in speaking, the former is pitched lower than the latter

(c) A person's name is always preceded by a 'u'. Tom is uTom, Jane is uJane, Sipho is uSipho, Gumede is uGumede

(d) Even though you identify the person doing the action, for instance: 'Joe smokes a lot' you must in Zulu use the personal Concord *in addition to* the name, so that this sentence will read:
  - Joe *he* smoke a lot = uJoe u- bhema kakhulu = UJoe ubhema kakhulu. This applies not only where a name is used but also to any word applicable to a person, e.g. 'a child' is umntwana. In the sentence 'the child cries a lot', the Zulu is
  - 'child *he* cry a lot' = umntwana u- khala kakhulu = Umntwana ukhala kakhulu

This also applies to the plural. The plural of umntwana is abantwana, so that the sentence: The children cry a lot, would be rendered in Zulu as:
  - children *they* cry a lot = abantwana ba- khala kakhulu = Abantwana bakhala kakhulu

Remember that every action requires two elements, the Concord (as the one who performs the action) and the verb (the action itself), and these form one word

(e) There is normally no difference between 'a' and 'the' (indefinite and definite), neither of which are expressed. 'A person needs food', and 'The person needs food' are expressed as: Person he need food = umuntu u-dinga ukudla = Umuntu udinga ukudla. Speakers of Fanakalo would do well to note this aspect — the use of 'lo' before every noun in Fanakalo, e.g. lo inja, lo muntu, lo sinkwa is entirely wrong. Similarly, 'some' is not expressed. 'I want some bread' is merely: I want bread = ngi- funa isinkwa = Ngifuna isinkwa

(f) Words which in English are used to assist a verb, such as: am, is, are, do, does, etc are not normally expressed in Zulu. The children play outside — the children are playing outside — the children do play outside would be: Children they play outside = abantwana ba-dlala phandle = Abantwana badlala phandle

▶ Now learn the following vocabulary:

### Verbs

| | |
|---|---|
| khuluma | talk |
| bona | see |
| khala | cry |
| siza | help |
| phuza | drink |
| funa | want |
| thanda | like, love |
| hamba | go, walk, proceed |
| bhema | smoke |
| sebenza | work |
| letha | bring |

### Nouns

| | |
|---|---|
| isinkwa | bread |
| ushukela | sugar |
| itiye | tea |
| umuntu | a person |
| abantu | people |
| uDlamini | a common surname |
| inja | dog |
| ubisi | milk |
| ubaba | father |
| umntwana | child |
| abantwana | children |

### Others

| | |
|---|---|
| kahle | well, nicely |
| lapha | here |
| eThekwini | in, at, to, from Durban |
| manje | now |
| phandle | outside |
| kakhulu | greatly, a lot, much, very |

*Some examples:*

○ I want Tom    ngi-funa uTom = Ngifuna uTom
   They like tea    ba- thanda itiye = Bathanda itiye
○ We work here    si- sebenza lapha = Sisebenza lapha
○ You (plural) talk a lot    ni-khuluma kakhulu = Nikhuluma kakhulu
○ You (singular) talk a lot    u- khuluma kakhulu = Ukhuluma kakhulu
○ The child is drinking milk
   Umntwana u-phuza ubisi = Umntwana uphuza ubisi
○ The people want bread    abantu ba- funa isinkwa = Abantu bafuna isinkwa

## 3. Incomplete actions

As has been shown, an action requires two elements — the Concord and the verb-, but whereas in English this can form a sentence, in Zulu it is regarded as incomplete and they complete it by inserting -ya- between the two. 'I see' would not be left as ngi- bona but becomes: ngi- ya bona to form one word = ngiyabona. 'Tom sees' would not be: uTom u- bona but would be: uTom u- ya bona = UTom uyabona.

The rule is that if there is no word following the action, use -ya-, but if there is such a word, do not use -ya-.

*Examples:*
○    We work = si + ya + sebenza = Siyasebenza:
○    We work well = Sisebenza kahle:    They are talking = ba + ya + khuluma = Bayakhuluma:    They talk a lot = Bakhuluma kakhulu
○    Joe is talking = uJoe u + ya + khuluma = UJoe uyakhuluma
○    Joe talks a lot = UJoe ukhuluma kakhulu

Also, when an action comes at the end of a sentence (i.e. has no word following) you use -ya- e.g.

Joyce is drinking tea but Mary is working = UJoyce uphuza itiye kodwa uMary uyasebenza.

There is no special meaning to attach to this -ya- in the context stated, it is simply a third element in an action in the present tense which is otherwise regarded as incomplete. The impression must not be given that *every* sentence in Zulu requires three elements. There are many which consist of only two elements, e.g. si + khona = sikhona (we are here), ba + phi = baphi? (where are they?). It is only an *action* (i.e. a verb) that takes 'ya' if no word follows e.g. bayadlala (they are playing) compared to bakhona (they are here).

*Some sentences* (Applying our knowledge up to this stage):
○    We work in Durban    Sisebenza eThekwini
○    Joyce is bringing sugar    UJoyce uletha ushukela
○    The people are going    Abantu bayahamba
○    Jacob smokes    UJacob uyabhema
○    Jacob smokes a lot    UJacob ubhema kakhulu
○    Peter wants bread now    UPeter ufuna isinkwa manje
○    Joseph is helping father but Dick is crying
     UJoseph usiza ubaba kodwa uDick uyakhala

Complete the following sentences:
1.   They are drinking tea    —— phuza itiye
2.   He likes the dog    —— thanda inja
3.   Tom is working    UTom —— sebenza
4.   Father is helping the children    Ubaba —— siza abantwana
5.   The people want bread    Abantu —— funa isinkwa
6.   Joe is bringing the milk but I am going    UJoe —— letha ubisi kodwa —— hamba

7. You (singular) smoke a lot —— bhema kakhulu
8. You (plural) talk a lot —— khuluma kakhulu
Answers: 1. ba 2. u 3. u ya 4. u 5. ba 6. u ngi ya 7. u 8. ni

▶ *Vocabulary*
Now learn the following words:
*Verbs*

| | |
|---|---|
| geza | wash |
| biza | call, summon |
| lala | sleep, lie down |
| dlala | play |
| hlala | stay (reside), sit |
| dla | eat |
| pheka | cook |
| funda | learn, read |

*Nouns*

| | |
|---|---|
| inyama | meat |
| amanzi | water |
| umfowethu | my brother |
| abafowethu | my brothers |
| amaswidi | sweets |
| ikhofi | coffee |
| isiZulu | the Zulu language |
| isiNgisi | the English language |

*Other*

| | |
|---|---|
| kodwa | but |
| yebo | yes |
| phakathi | inside |
| ekhishini | in the kitchen |
| ebhange | to, from, at the bank |
| engadini | in the garden |
| eMlazi | at, to, from Umlazi |
| kancane | a little |
| cha | no |
| ekhaya | at, to from home |
| ebusuku | at night |
| emini | during the day |
| eposini | to, from, at the post office |

## 4. *Questions: General*

In English we put the question word (interrogative) first, e.g. *What* do you see? *Where* is he going? *Why* do you smoke? but in Zulu you turn the word order around to start with the person doing the action, so that the above queries would be rendered as:
You see what (Ubonani)?   He go where (Uyaphi)?
You smoke why (Ubhemelani)?

5

Guard against a literal translation from the English (such as in Fanakalo, e.g. Yini wena bona = What do you see?)

## General Questions

Apart from special interrogative words such as who, what, where, when, how, etc (all of which are found in Zulu), any statement can be turned into a question by placing NA at the end and this I call a General question. Remember that words like 'do', 'is', 'are' which are used in English to begin a question are not used in Zulu, and here again (as in most Zulu sentences) you start with the person doing the action, e.g. Do you stay here? is rendered as: You stay here NA = Uhlala lapha na? Are the children playing outside? becomes: Children they play outside NA = Abantwana badlala phandle na? Is Tom going? becomes: Tom he go NA = UTom uyahamba na?

Some examples of statements turned into questions:

- You are drinking tea   Uphuza itiye
- Are you drinking tea?   Uphuza itiye na?
- He likes meat   Uthanda inyama
- Does he like meat?   Uthanda inyama na?

  Mary is cooking potatoes   UMary upheka amazambane
  Is Mary cooking potatoes?   UMary upheka amazambana na?

Note that as in English, you can of course also indicate a question, when speaking, by the inflexion of your voice, and if you do this, the use of NA at the end is optional.

Note too that the query NA is not regarded as a *word* but is merely an expression indicating a question (i.e. a question mark that is spoken), hence a sentence incorporating -ya- (see para 3) still retains the -ya- if the query NA is added e.g.

- He is working = Uyasebenza
- Is he working = Uyasebenza na?


## 5.   Replies

Standard replies are:  Yes = Yebo   No = Cha

## Some Examples:

- Do you smoke? (you smoke NA)= Uyabhema na?
- Yes, I smoke = Yebo, ngiyabhema
- Does Joe work? (Joe he work NA) = UJoe uyasebenza na?
- Yes, he works in Durban = Yebo, usebenza eThekwini
  Is Father going now? (father he go now NA) = Ubaba uhamba manje na?
  No, he is eating = Cha, uyadla
- Are the people eating meat? (people they eat meat NA)? = Abantu badla inyama na?
- No, they are drinking tea = Cha, baphuza itiye

## Exercise No. 1

(a) *Translate into Zulu:*
1. I see a dog  2. We like milk  3. John works in Durban  4. They are cooking meat  5. Father is washing  6. I am eating  7. You sleep a lot  8. They are calling George  9. We play during the day  10. He is crying

(b) *Translate into English:*
1. Ngithanda isinkwa kakhulu  2. UMary uphuza ubisi  3. Bahlala eMlazi  4. Bayadlala  5. UAnnie uletha itiye  6. Ufunda kahle  7. Umntwana uyadla  8. Ubaba ufuna umsebenzi  9. Ngiyageza  10. ULettie upheka inyama

(c) *Translate into Zulu:*
1. Do you stay at Umlazi?  2. No, I stay at KwaMashu  3. Is George working?  4. Yes, he is working  5. Do they drink tea a lot?  6. No, they like milk  7. Do you work?  8. No, I am looking for (= want) work  9. Is Mary cooking meat?  10. No, she is eating bread

(d) *Translate into English:*
1. Uyasebenza na?  2. Yebo, ngisebenza eThekwini  3. Abantwana badlala kahle na?  4. Yebo, badlala kahle  5. UDlamini udla inyama na?  6. Yebo, uthanda inyama kakhulu  7. UMary uletha itiye na?  8. Cha, uletha ikhofi  9. Uthanda uKhumalo na?  10. Cha, ngithanda uDlamini

# CHAPTER TWO

Conjunctions (But, And/Also, Because, Or)
Infinitive (to . . .)

## 6. *Conjunctions*

Study the following sentences:

Joe likes tea but Tom likes coffee.
UJoe uthanda itiye kodwa uTom uthanda ikhofi.

We sleep during the day because we work at night.
Silala emini ngoba sisebenza ebusuku.

I work in Durban but father stays at home.
Ngisebenza eThekwini kodwa ubaba uhlala ekhaya.

I work but father stays at home.
Ngiyasebenza kodwa ubaba uhlala ekhaya.

Conjunctions join complete sentences, each of which can stand on its own. Note that because the sentences on both sides of the conjunction are independent and do not form part of each other, the conjunction itself is not regarded as a 'following word', hence the first sentence must incorporate -ya- if it has no following word (apart from the conjunction and the sentence that follows it). The last sentence above is an example.

(a) **but    kodwa**
  ○    Jim works during the day but Dick works at night
       UJim usebenza emini kodwa uDick usebenza ebusuku

       I am reading but Mary is cooking meat
       Ngiyafunda kodwa uMary upheka inyama

---

**Key to Symbols in text** to be used in conjunction with tapes:
  ○    The word or sentence
  ▷    The complete line
  ▶    The complete section

(b) **and/also    futhi**   This word also means: Besides, too, again, etc.
    We work and we study at night
    Siyasebenza futhi sifunda ebusuku

- o   They drink tea, they also like coffee
      Baphuza itiye futhi bathanda ikhofi

It is not uncommon for 'futhi' to be placed at the end, and the above sentence could have read: Baphuza itiye, bathanda ikhofi futhi. Note also that 'futhi' is here used to join sentences. The word 'and' when joining things, names, etc. is dealt with later (para 30).

(c) **because    ngoba**
- o   We work because we want money
      Siyasebenza ngoba sifuna imali

- o   I drink milk because I like to ('to' is not expressed)
      Ngiphuza ubisi ngoba ngiyathanda

(d) **or    noma**
    He is reading or he is drinking tea
    Uyafunda noma uphuza itiye

- o   Does George work in Durban or (does he) stay at home?
      UGeorge usebenza eThekwini noma uhlala ekhaya na?

Noma can also be used between nouns, adverbs etc. and not only sentences

e.g.   James or John    UJames noma uJohn
       tea or coffee    itiye noma ikhofi
       yes or no    yebo noma cha
       outside or inside    phandle noma phakathi

Now learn the following vocabulary:

*Verbs*

|   |   |
|---|---|
| thatha | take |
| fika | come, arrive |
| buya | return |
| zama | try |
| thenga | buy |
| vula | open |

*Nouns*

|   |   |
|---|---|
| umsebenzi | employment, job |
| umfana | boy |
| abafana | boys |
| ibhuku | book |
| ikati | cat |
| amazambane | potatoes |
| ugwayi | tobacco |

*Other*

| | | |
|---|---|---|
| o | phambili | in front |
| o | emuva | behind |
| o | esitolo | at, to, from the shop |
| o | lapho | there (near you) |
| o | mhlawumbe | perhaps |
| o | esikoleni | at, to, from school |
| o | angazi | I don't know |
| o | namuhla (namhlanje) | today |
| o | ehhovisi | to, at, in the office |

## 7. Infinitives

Study the following sentences:

I want sugar    Ngifuna ushukela
I want to buy sugar    Ngifuna ukuthenga ushukela
Children like sweets    Abantwana bathanda amaswidi
Children like to eat sweets    Abantwana bathanda ukudla amaswidi

The word 'to', called the infinitive, is UKU-. It is the link between verbs such as: want, like, try etc. and the action desired by the speaker, exactly as in English. It cannot, however, stand alone, but is joined to the action word (verb) following it.

*Examples*:
The people like to stay here    Abantu bathanda ukuhlala lapha

o   Joe wants to go now    UJoe ufuna ukuhamba manje

o   We are trying to learn Zulu    Sizama ukufunda isiZulu

Do not confuse this word 'to' with the word indicating direction (preposition) e.g. they are going to school, which is dealt with later under the heading of Locatives.

Note also that the infinitive 'to' now under discussion applies when the speaker desires to do some action himself. It does not apply if the desired action is to be done by someone else e.g. I want *you* to go   or   I want *him* to go (see paragraph 46).

*General Note re Verbs*
By now it will be seen that an action word (verb) never stands by itself, except in one instance (shown below). It is always combined with a preceding concord (ngi- u- u- etc.) or with the infinitive uku-. Guard against the following mistakes often made by beginners:

Joe works here
   *Wrong* UJoe sebenza lapha    *Right* UJoe *u*sebenza lapha
I want to go
   *Wrong* Ngifuna hamba    *Right* Ngifuna *uku*hamba

The one exception is in the case of a command e.g. Vula! Open! which is dealt with in paragraph 12.

# Exercise No. 2

(a) *Translate into Zulu*

1. We are working but Tom is washing. 2. Joe likes tea and he (also) likes milk. 3. I wash in the morning but George washes at night. 4. They are calling John, they also want Sipho. 5. Lettie is crying because she wants sweets. 6. Do you want to work or do you want to play? 7. We like to eat meat but they like to drink tea. 8. I want to sleep now. 9. Dudu is crying because she wants to drink some milk. 10. They like to work in Durban.

(b) *Translate into English:*

1. Ngiyageza kodwa uJoseph uphuza itiye. 2. Bafuna itiye, futhi bafuna isinkwa. 3. Uthanda itiye noma ubisi na? 4. Ngigeza ekuseni ngoba ngisebenza emini. 5. uJoyce ufuna ukupheka inyama. 6. Uthanda inyama na? 7. Yebo, ngithanda inyama futhi ngithanda isinkwa. 8. UJoe uthanda ukuhlala ekhaya kodwa ngithanda ukusebenza. 9. UMary uletha itiye noma ubisi na? 10. Sizama ukufunda isiZulu.

(c) *Complete the following sentences and give their translations:*

1. UDick -phuza itiye (but) uJoseph -dlala phandle 2. (We want) -thenga amazambane esitolo 3. Umntwana (likes) amaswidi 4. Uyasebenza (or do you) -hlala ekhaya na? 5. (The children are crying) ngoba (they want some milk) 6. (Do you want) ukuhlala (here)? 7. Abafana -thanda -dlala kakhulu 8. Sithanda (to learn) isiZulu ngoba (we want to speak) kahle 9. (Do they like) itiye (or) ikhofi na? 10. Ngithenga inyama esitolo (also I am buying) isinkwa.

# CHAPTER THREE

### More questions: What? Where? Why?
### To be present/not present

## 8. More about questions

Study the following sentences:
Do you stay here?    Uhlala lapha na?
Where do you stay?    Uhlalaphi?

Is she buying bread?    Uthenga isinkwa na?
What is she buying?    Uthengani?

Does Tom work at night?    UTom usebenza ebusuku na?
Why does Tom work at night?    UTom usebenzelani ebusuku?

Are they studying?    Bayafunda na?
What are they studying?    Bafundani?

He is eating    Uyadla
Where is he eating?    Udlaphi?

The children are crying    Abantwana bayakhala
Why are the children crying?    Abantwana bakhalelani?

The following observations arise from the above:
(a) An interrogative is itself a word which asks a question, so that the addition of
    NA at the end (which indicates a general question) is unnecessary. It can,
    however, be used if you wish, and is often used if special emphasis is desired.
(b) The 'ya' which is used to complete a short statement (see para 3) is NEVER
    used with any interrogative. In this respect it differs from the General question
    NA which as we have stated is really only a spoken question mark.
(c) In speaking, the stress is on the syllable before the last, so that by adding a
    syllable to form the question, the stress in the verb is moved along accordingly
    e.g. uya*la*la becomes ula*la*phi?
    Note that it is only the three interrogatives What? Where? and Why? that are
    formed in this manner. All the others are separate words and are dealt with later.

---

**Key to Symbols in text** to be used in conjunction with tapes:
○    The word or sentence
▷    The complete line
►    The complete section

## 9. Questions: What? Where? Why?

*WHAT?*    Add -NI to the verb

○   What are they reading? ( = They read what?)    Bafunda + -ni = Bafundani?

*WHERE?*    Add -PHI to the verb

○   Where does Joe work? (Joe he work where?)   UJoe usebenza + -phi = UJoe usebenzaphi

*WHY?*    Add -ELANI to the verb (after dropping the final 'a' of the verb)

○   Why are you crying? (You cry why)   Ukhala + -elani = ukhal + elani = Ukhalelani?

Now learn the following the following new vocabulary:

*Verbs*

| | | |
|---|---|---|
| ○ | hleka | laugh |
| ○ | cela | request, ask for |
| ○ | thola | get |
| | shesha | hurry |
| | baleka | run away |
| | nika | give |
| ○ | ya | go towards (with destination stated) |
| | sika | cut |
| ○ | gijima | run |

*Nouns*

| | | |
|---|---|---|
| | imali | money |
| ○ | uthisha | teacher |
| ○ | utshwala | beer |
| | izitsha | dishes |
| | utshani | grass |
| ○ | udokotela | doctor |

*Others*

| | | |
|---|---|---|
| ○ | kusasa | tomorrow |
| ○ | endlini | in, to, from house |
| ○ | phezulu | on top |
| ○ | ntambama | in the afternoon |
| ○ | kabi | badly |
| ○ | esibhedlela | in, to, from hospital |

## 10. Above questions preceded by infinitive

In a question such as: What do you want to buy? remember that the question additives -ni, -phi and -elani are attached to the action that is being queried and not to the 'want'. The translation will therefore be: You want . . . to buy what? = ufuna uku- thenga -ni = Ufuna ukuthengani? The mistake commonly made (ufunani ukuthenga) can be avoided by remembering always to rephrase your sentence to start with the person doing the action, followed by the verb of wanting/desiring/trying, then linking it by uku- to the desired action which has the query added at the end.

*Examples:*

    *What ? -NI*

    What do they like to eat? = They like . . . to eat what?

    Bathanda . . . ukudlani = Bathanda ukudlani?

o    What are you trying to learn? = You try . . . to learn what?

    Uzama . . . ukufundani = Uzama ukufundani?

    *Where ? -PHI*

o    Where do you want to sit? = You want . . . to sit where?

    Ufuna . . . uku- hlala -phi = Ufuna ukuhlalaphi?

    Where do they like to play? = They like . . . to play where?

    Bathanda . . . uku-dlala -phi = Bathanda ukudlalaphi?

    *Why ? -ELANI*

    This instance is an exception and it is permissible to use both forms

o    Why does Joe want to go? = Joe he want . . . to go why?

    uJoe ufuna . . . uku-hamb-elani = UJoe ufuna ukuhambelani?

    OR

    Joe he want why . . . to go?

    uJoe ufun-elani . . . uku-hamba = UJoe ufunelani ukuhamba?

    Why do the children like to cry? = Children they like . . . to cry why?

    OR

    they like why . . . to cry?

    Abantwana bathanda ukukhalelani?

    OR

    Bathandelani ukukhala?

## 11. *To be present/not present*

Now examine the following sentences, which concern the question 'where':

o    Where do the children play? = Children they play where?

    Abantwana badlalaphi?

o    Where are the children? = Children they where?

    Abantwana baphi?

o    Where is Joe working? = Joe he work where?

    UJoe usebenzaphi?

o    Where is Joe? = Joe he where?

    UJoe uphi?

It will be seen that -phi can be added on not only to a verb, which queries where an *action* is taking place, but also to a concord, which queries the *whereabouts* of the person. In the latter instance, the concord can be regarded as having the meaning 'to be' i.e. ngi- means not only I, but also 'I am': u- means you, you are: u- means he/she, he is/she is, etc. By adding -phi to the pronoun u- you therefore get the meaning: he is where? and this is the method of asking whereabouts of a person.

    (a)   *Use of KHONA*

        If the reply is: He is here, he is present, the word 'khona' is used together with the concord ('khona' means: present, here, available)

*Examples*:

Where is Tom?    uTom u- + -phi = UTom uphi?
He is here    u- + khona = Ukhona

o    Where are you?    U + phi? = Uphi?
o    I am here    Ngi- + khona = Ngikhona (i.e. I am present)
o    Where are the people today?    Abantu ba- + phi namuhla = Abantu baphi namuhla?
o    They are present    Ba- + khona = Bakhona

'Khona' can also be used to ask a general question regarding whereabouts without specifically asking where the person is.

*Examples:*

o    Is Peter here? = Peter he present    NA = UPeter ukhona na?
o    Yes, he is present = Yebo, ukhona.
o    Are the children present? = children they present    NA = Abantwana bakhona na?
o    Yes, they are present    Yebo, bakhona

If the reply is in the negative, the replies are:

He is not here    Akekho (some say Akakho)
They are not here    Abekho (some say Abakho)

(The grammatical explanation of the above will be given at a later stage)

*Example:*

Is Tom here?    UTom ukhona na?
No, he is not    Cha, akekho

o    Are the chidren here today?    Abantwana bakhona namuhla na?
o    No, they are absent    Cha, abekho
o    Where is Dick today?    UDick uphi namuhla?
o    I don't know, he is not here    Angazi, akekho

(b)    *Specific Whereabouts*
   (a)    Whereas 'khona' is used to indicate that a person is present or not, it is not used (unless special emphasis is required) if the *actual place* is given. In this case, the concord is used by itself together with the place in question e.g.
   I am inside = I inside = ngi- + phakathi = Ngiphakathi.
   They are in front = they in front = ba- + phambili = Baphambili
   There is one item to remember in this connection, however, and that is if the place begins with an 'E' (as are most Locatives, see para 35), a 'cushion' must be used between the concord and such word, the reason being that two vowels may not be placed next to each other in one word, hence they are separated by a 'cushion' the sound of which is usually represented by the letter 'S' e.g.
   I am inside = ngiphakathi but: I am in the house = ngi + s + endlini = Ngisendlini
   They are at school = ba + s + esikoleni = Basesikoleni
   Where is Jane? She (is) at home = UJane uphi? U + s + ekhaya = Usekhaya
   (b)    In the negative, however, there is no question of a 'cushion' because the words akekho and abekho (he is not present/they are not present)

15

are words that stand on their own, hence there is no question of two vowels following each other in one word. The word describing the place is used after akekho/abekho, whether or not it starts with an 'E' e.g.

He is not at home = Akekho ekhaya

He is not here = Akekho lapha

They are not at school = Abekho esikoleni

▶ Now translate the following sketch (of foreman A and his induna B):

A: Abantu bakhona namuhla na?

B: Yebo, bakhona, kodwa hhayi bonke (not all)

A: UGumede ukhona na?

B: Yebo, ukhona

A: UDuma ukhona na?

B: Cha, akekho

A: Uphi?

B: Angazi, mhlawumbe uyagula

A: UDuma uhlalaphi?

B: Uhlala eMlazi

A: Usekhaya na?

B: Angazi, mhlawumbe usesibhedlela ngoba uyagula

A: Kulungile, masihambe manje

Answer to above:

A: Are the people here today?

B: Yes, they are here, but not all.

A: Is Gumede here?

B: Yes, he is here.

A: Is Duma here?

B: No, he is not here.

A: Where is he?

B: I don't know, perhaps he is ill.

A: Where does Duma stay?

B: He stays at Umlazi.

A: Is he at home?

B: I don't know, perhaps he is at the hospital because he is ill.

A: OK let us go now.

## Exercise No. 3

(a) *Translate into Zulu:*

1. What does Joe want? 2. What are they reading? 3. What is the child eating? 4. What do you like to drink? 5. What is Jane bringing now? 6. What is the child asking for? 7. What do you like to read at night? 8. Does George like to work in the day or does he like to work at night? 9. What do you see over there? 10. What are they bringing today?

(b) *Translate into English:*

1. UMary uphekani manje? 2. UGeorge uthanda ukudlani? 3. Abantu bafundani? 4. Abantu bathengani esitolo? 5. UJoseph ufuna ukufundani ekhaya? 6. Ubaba uthanda ukuphuzani ebusuku? 7. Ubonani lapho phandle? 8. UJane ugezani ekhishini? 9. Abantu badlani ekhaya, futhi baphuzani? 10. Ufunani lapha?

(c) *Translate into Zulu:*

1. Where do you sleep at night? 2. Where are the children playing? 3. Where do you like to stay? 4. Where do they want to work? 5. Is Joe present? Yes, he is. 6. But where is he? He is in the garden. 7. Where are the children? 8. They are playing outside in the garden. 9. Are the people here today? No, they are not. 10. Where are they? They are at home.

(d) *Translate into English:*

1. Uhlalaphi manje? 2. Abantu bathanda ukusebenzaphi? 3. UMary uphekaphi inyama? Upheka ekhishini. 4. Abantu basekhaya. 5. UGeorge uphi? Uphandle. 6. Abantu basemsebenzini (at work) na? 7. Yebo, basemsebenzini. 8. Abantwana baphi? Baphandle. 9. UJoseph ukhona namuhla na? Cha, akekho. 10. Uphi? Angazi

(e) *Translate into Zulu:*

1. Why do we work? 2. We work because we want money. 3. Why is the child laughing? Because he sees the cat. 4. Why do the people want money? 5. Because they want to buy some bread. 6. Why do they learn Zulu? 7. Because they want to speak well. 8. Why do you like to sleep during the day? 9. Because I work at night. 10. Why do they want to run away? Because they see the dog.

(f) *Translate into English:*

1. Ulethelani imali? 2. Ngoba ngifuna ukunika uJoe imali. 3. Usebenzelani ebusuku? 4. Ngoba ngithola imali kakhulu. 5. Abantwana bafunelani ukuhamba manje? 6. Ngoba bafuna ukudlala ibhola (football). 7. UJoe uthandelani ukufunda ebusuku? 8. Ngoba usebenza emini. 9. Umntwana ubalekelani? 10. Ubaleka ngoba ubona inyoka (snake).

# CHAPTER FOUR

Commands
Instructions and Requests
Negative thereof

Learn the following new vocabulary:

*Verbs*

| | | |
|---|---|---|
| o | beka | put, place |
| | shanela | sweep |
| o | qala | begin, start |
| | vala | shut |
| | vuka | wake up, arise |
| o | qeda | finish, complete |
| | sula | wipe, clean |
| | lungisa | prepare, correct |
| o | phumula | rest |
| o | susa | remove |
| o | lalela | listen, obey |
| o | buza | ask, enquire |
| o | buka | look at |
| | landa | fetch |
| | jabula | be happy, rejoice |
| o | tshela | tell |
| o | khombisa | show |
| | phuma | come out, go out |

*Miscellaneous*

| | | |
|---|---|---|
| | umnyango | door |
| | ibhakede | bucket |
| o | ngokushesha | fast |
| o | phansi | below |
| | itafula | table |
| | ekamelweni | in, to, from the room |
| o | masinyane | soon |
| o | lokhu | this, this thing |

---

**Key to Symbols in text** to be used in conjunction with tapes:
   o    The word or sentence
   ▷    The complete line
   ►    The complete section

## 12. Commands

    Now study the following:
- Come back!   Buya!
  Come back here!   Buya lapha!
- Come back, I say!   Buya -bo!
- Joseph, come back here   Joseph, buya lapha
- You there Joseph, come back here   We Joseph, buya lapha
  (You there) child, come back here   (We) mntwana, buya lapha
- Children, come back here   Bantwana, buyani lapha
  I want you (singular) to come back here   Ngifuna (ukuthi) ubuye lapha
  I want you (plural) to come back here   Ngifuna (ukuthi) nibuye lapha
  Please come back here (one person)   Ngicela (ukuthi) ubuye lapha
  Please come back here (plural)   Ngicela (ukuthi) nibuye lapha
- OK, you may go/very well, go then   Hamba -ke.
  A study of the above shows the following features:
  1. In a command (imperative), the verb is used by itself without a concord e.g. Hamba! Go!   Letha imali! Bring the money!
  2. When addressing someone, the first vowel of the name or noun is dropped: uTom becomes Tom! umntwana becomes mntwana! abantwana becomes bantwana!
  3. If you wish to draw the attention of the person addressed, use WE (pronounced as in 'wet') before the name. This word can be used for both one person or more than one e.g. We mfana! You boy!   We bafana! You boys!
  4. If more than one person is being addressed, add -NI to the verb e.g. hambani! (to more than one person)   Buyani kusasa! Come back tomorrow (more than one)
  5. The addition of -BO (singular or plural) expresses insistence, urgency etc.
     - Khuluma -bo! Speak up, you must speak!
       Khulumani -bo! Speak up! (to more than one)
  6. The use of -KE has a 'softening' effect and implies permission to do the act e.g.
     hamba-ke = go then, you may go, it's in order to go, etc.
     hambani-ke = go then, you may go, etc. (to more than one person)
     It is often used after Kulungile (meaning: very well, it is in order) e.g.
     - Kulungile, letha-ke imali kusasa
       It's all right, bring the money tomorrow.

## 13. Instructions and requests

1. Instructions, introduced by 'ngifuna' (I want) and requests, introduced by 'ngicela' (I request) are followed by the action required or requested with the Concord u- or ni- (denoting singular or plural) but the verb of such action ends in -e. A word that is usually omitted but can be used if desired is 'ukuthi' meaning: 'that' e.g.
   - I want that you return tomorrow
     Ngifuna ukuthi ubuye kusasa

   ○    I want you return tomorrow
         Ngifuna ubuye kusasa
         (= I want you to return tomorrow)
         I request that you shut the door    Ngicela ukuthi uvale umnyango
         I request you shut the door    Ngicela uvale umnyango

2. The word, 'please', for which no direct equivalent exists in Zulu, is rendered by the foregoing 'ngicela u . . .-e' e.g. Please bring the tea = I request you bring tea = Ngicela ulethe itiye

(There are other ways of expressing 'please' but this is one of the most common)

Examples of the foregoing:
   ○    Call Joseph    Biza uJoseph
         Help the child    Siza umntwana
         Be quiet, you (shut up!)    Thula-bo!
   ○    Gumede, tell the people    Gumede, tshela abantu
         You there my brother, come here    We mfowethu, woza lapha
         Chidren, study well    Bantwana, fundani kahle
         I want you (to) call the children    Ngifuna ubize abantwana
   ○    Please open the door    Ngicela uvule umnyango


## 14. Multiple commands, instructions and requests

*Commands*: If a series of commands is given, the first is in the Command form (i.e. verb alone) while the second and subsequent commands take the form of straight sentences but with the verb ending in -e, e.g.
   ○    Go now and come back tomorrow ('and' is not expressed)
         Hamba manje . . . ubuye kusasa    Go now, you return tomorrow
         Hamba manje ubuye kusasa    Go now return tomorrow
   ○    Come and see = come you see = Woza ubone
         Hurry and return = hurry you return = Shesha ubuye (this is equivalent to: come back quickly)
      *Come back tomorrow, bring money and buy the clothes
      Buya kusasa ulethe imali uthenge izingubo

*Instructions/Requests*: A similar situation applies where there are a series of instructions or requests. After the initial 'ngifuna u . . .-e' (instruction) or 'ngicela u . . .-e' (request), all subsequent actions to be performed are merely a repetition of 'u . . .-e' (verb ends in -e) e.g.
*I want you to take the money, go now, and return tomorrow
Ngifuna uthathe imali uhambe manje ubuye kusasa

*Please tell the people, shut the door and come inside
Ngicela utshele abantu uvale umnyango ungene phakathi

A word often used in connection with multiple commands, instructions and requests is 'bese' meaning: and then. It is usually placed before the last action to be performed and is followed by a straight verb e.g. in above * sentences:

Come back tomorrow, bring money and buy the clothes
Buya kusasa ulethe imali bese uthenga izingubo

o I want you to take the money, go now and (then) return tomorrow
Ngifuna uthathe imali uhambe manje bese ubuya kusasa

o Please tell the people, shut the door and (then) come inside
Ngicela utshele abantu uvale umnyango bese ungena phakathi


## 15. Negative commands, instructions and requests

The word MUSA means: desist, stop doing, cease, do not etc. and is always followed by the infinitive UKU-. In Zulu, this would be: desist to, stop doing to, cease to, do not to, and so on, e.g.

▷ Hamba! Go!  Musa ukuhamba! Don't go!
In *spoken* Zulu the two words are often run into one, to form MUSUKU-

o Don't come tomorrow   Musukufika kusasa
Don't tell Joe   Musukutshela uJoe
but in the written form they are separate, as:
Musa ukufika kusasa, musa ukutshela uJoe
If addressing more than one person, add -NI to MUSA = Musani and this is still followed by uku- e.g.

o Children, don't hit the dog
Bantwana, musani ukushaya inja
You there, boys, don't look at the girls
We bafana, musani ukubuka amantombazane
The expression 'please don't' is rather involved to explain, but is not necessary as the use of 'Musa uku-...' is appropriate on all occasions where a negative command, instruction or request is being conveyed.

Note: See item 2 App II for another way to give a negative instruction.


## 16. Negative and positive commands, instructions and requests

Where a negative instruction is followed by a positive one, the latter may be given as an ordinary instruction or command, or it can take the form of: I want you to . . . Ngifuna u . . . -e, e.g.

o Don't go now, go this afternoon
Musa ukuhamba manje, hamba ntambama
OR

o Don't go now, I want you (to) go this afternoon
Musa ukuhamba manje, ngifuna uhambe ntambama
Note: There are other methods of expressing negative and positive instructions and requests but they are not dealt with in this course.

## Exercise No. 4

(a) *Translate into Zulu:*
1. Call the child now. 2. Please call the child now. 3. Mary, please call Joseph. 4. Joyce, sweep the office then tidy up (lungisa). 5. I want you to take the cheques, go to the bank then bring back some money. 6. Don't get petrol today. 7. Don't get oil at the garage, just get petrol. 8. I say, George, help the child over there. 9. Stop it, I say. 10. All right then, go now and come back tomorrow.

(b) *Translate into English:*
1. Ngifuna ushanele esitolo ekuseni. 2. Musa ukukhuluma kakhulu. 3. We Mary, ngicela ulethe itiye manje ngoba sifuna ukuya ebhange. 4. Dlamini, hamba manje ubuye ntambama ulethe imali. 5. Thula-bo! 6. Bantwana, fundani kahle ekhaya bese nibuya esikoleni kusasa. 7. Musa ukunika umntwana amaswidi, ufuna ubisi. 8. Vula ihhovisi ekuseni uvule futhi amafasitela (windows) bese uya eposini. 9. George, ngifuna ubuye ntambama. 10. Khumalo, musa ukuletha ibhuku ngifuna ulethe ipensele.

# CHAPTER FIVE

Greetings
Farewells
Salutations
Some useful phrases

## 17. *Learn the following vocabulary:*

○ bingelela       greet
    phila       be alive, be well
    bonga       thank, praise
    njani?       how, in what condition
    lungile       good, in order
    igama       name
    umnumzana       gentleman, sir
    inkosi       king, chief
    inkosazana       princess
○ valelisa       say farewell
    sala       remain, stay
    dinga       need, require
    ku-       'it' (indefinite)
    kunjalo       it is so, it is like that
    isibongo       surname
    inkosikazi       madam, queen
    inkosana       prince
    umngane       friend
    abangane       friends

*General Greeting*
○ To one person:    Sawubona or Sakubona
(a contraction of si (we) ya (do) ku (you) bona (see) = we see you)

This is a general greeting — good-morning, good-day, hullo, etc. — and is used at any time of day or night, and also on the phone.
○ To more than one person:    Sanibona or Sanibonani

*Examples:*
○   Good-morning George    Sawubona George
○   Good-morning Mr Duma    Sawubona mnumzana Duma

---

**Key to Symbols in text** to be used in conjunction with tapes:
     ○    The word or sentence
     ▷    The complete line
     ►    The complete section

o    Good-morning Mrs Duma    Sawubona nkosikazi Duma
o    Good-morning men    Sanibona madoda
o    Good-morning friends    Sanibona bangane

*General Reply:*
Yes, good-morning, hullo etc.    Yebo, sawubona (or sakubona)
*Examples:*
Yebo, sawubona mnumzana (sir) nkosikazi (madam)  Mnumzana Jones
(Mr Jones)   Eric, Joyce etc.
After above reply it is usual to ask after a person's health or well-being, the
standard question being:
o    Unjani? (made up of u- (you) + -njani (in what condition)
     or
o    Unjani wena? = How are *you*?
     Standard replies:
▷    Ngiyaphila   or   Ngisaphila   or   Sikhona/Ngikhona
     I am alive (well)   I am still well   We are around/I am around
     and this is usually followed by an enquiry as to the other party's health i.e.
▷    Unjani wena?   or   Wena-ke?   or   Ngingezwa ngawe
     How are *you*?        And you?        May I hear about you?
     Replies to above:
▷    Nami ngiyaphila   or   Nami ngisaphila   or   Nami ngikhona/Nathi sikhona
     I too am well                I too am still well        I too am around/we are around
     or perhaps:
     Angiphilile          or   Ngiyagula
     I am not well             I am sick      (See also item 3 App II re ill-health)
     It is often good to ask how *things* are, in addition to (or instead of) the state of
     health, e.g.
o    Kunjani?   How are things, howzit? (Made up of ku-(it) + -njani)
     Kunjani ekhaya?   How goes it at home?
     Reply to above:
o    Kulungile = it is all right (ku- + lungile)
o    Kuhamba kahle = it goes well
*Note*:  Except for the general greeting you can have any number of variations to the
     above.
*General Farewell, Goodbye*
Said by the person leaving:
o    Sala kahle (to one person)   or   Usale kahle
     Salani kahle (more than one)   or   Nisale kahle
     Stay well or may you stay well
     Said by the person remaining:
o    Hamba kahle (one person)   or   Uhambe kahle
     Hambani kahle (more than one) or   Nihambe kahle
     Go well                                  May you go well

## 18. Useful phrases

o  Thank you    Ngiyabonga (lit. I praise, I am grateful)
   Please    Ngicela u- . . . -e (I request you . . .)    or    Ake . . . u . . . (See item 4 App
   II)

o  Excuse me (e.g. to a stranger)    Uxolo
   Beg pardon, sorry!    Nxephe, nxese

   I am sorry (for a wrongful action)    Ngiyaxolisa
   (expressing sympathy)    Ngiyadabuka

   I am pleased to meet you
   Ngiyajabula (or ngiyathokoza) ukukwazi

   May we meet again    Sophinda sibonane
   I have just started to learn Zulu    Ngisaqala ukufunda isiZulu
o  I am still learning Zulu    Ngisafunda isiZulu
   I need to practise Zulu    Ngidinga ukuzijwayeza isiZulu

   Please help me and correct mistakes
   Ngicela ungisize ulungise amaphutha

o  Please speak slowly
   Ngicela ukhulume ungasheshisi

o  If you speak fast I cannot understand what you say
   Uma ukhuluma ngokushesha angizwa okushoyo

o  Do you speak English?    Uyasazi isiNgisi na?
   or    Uyakwazi ukukhuluma isiNgisi na?

   How do you say in Zulu . . . (whatever)?
   Kuthiwani ngesiZulu . . . (then the English you want translated)
   Come in    Ngena    or    ngena phakathi
   Sit down
   Hlala    or    Hlala phansi    or    Ungahlala/ngicela uhlale
   Sit            Sit down            You may sit/please be seated

   Would you like tea?
   Uthanda itiye na?    or    Ungaphuza itiye na?
   Yes please
   Yebo    or    Ngiyalithanda
   No thanks
   Ngiyabonga    or    Cha, ngiyabonga
   (Note that this expression is used to indicate *refusal* i.e. thank you for asking)
   Bonga ukudla = refuse food

   Come here    Woza    or    Woza lapha
   Come nearer    Sondela
o  What is your name?    Ungubani igama lakho?
   What is your surname?    Isibongo sakho ngubani?
   My name/surname is Joseph Gumede    Ngingu Joseph Gumede
   How old are you?    Uneminyaka emingaki?

Where are you from?   Uphumaphi?   or   Uvelaphi?
Do you speak English?   Uyasazi isiNgisi na?

○   What's the matter, what's wrong, what happened?
Kwenzenjani?   or   Kwenzekeni?

○   What did you say?   Utheni?
What do you say/think?   Uthini?
What are you doing?   Wenzani?
(Also means: what is he/she doing?)
Don't do this (again)
Musa ukwenza njalo   or   (Unga phinde wenze lokho)
Please don't!   Musa-bo!
I don't care   Anginandaba
That is so   Kunjalo
Is that so?   Kunjalo na?
Do you understand? (= Do you hear?)   Uyezwa na?
I understand   Ngiyezwa
○   What is this?   Yini lena?   or   Yini lokhu?

Some terms used in the domestic situation (real meanings given in the vocabulary above) are: The man of the house, sir — umnumzana   the wife, madam — inkosikazi   the son — inkosana   the daughter — inkosazana   the words ubasi (the boss) and umesisi (the madam) are in common use to describe the employer. The word 'intombazana' really means a girl, but is widely used to describe any female in domestic service, irrespective of age.

The word 'umfazi' (woman) should never be used as it has acquired a derogatory meaning.

Now attempt the following sketch concerning two friends, Sipho and Mandla (these are common male names — Sipho (a gift) Mandla (strength)).

▶   *Abangane: uSipho noMandla*

MANDLA:   Sawubona, Sipho
SIPHO:   Yebo, sawubona Mandla
MANDLA:   Unjani?
SIPHO:   Ngiyaphila. Unjani wena?
MANDLA:   Nami ngisaphila. Kunjani ekhaya?
SIPHO:   Ekhaya kulungile kodwa ubaba uyagula.
MANDLA:   Ngiyadabuka ukuzwa (to hear) lokho. Ugula kakhulu, okusho ukuthi usesibhedlela na? (okusho ukuthi = that means to say, that is)
SIPHO:   Cha, akekho esibhedlela, uphuza imithi (medicines) ekhaya. Uyaphi manje Mandla?
MANDLA:   Ngiya esitolo, ngifuna ukuthenga.
SIPHO:   Ufuna ukuthengani esitolo?
MANDLA:   Ekhaya sidinga isinkwa, sidinga futhi itiye.
SIPHO:   Nami ngifuna ukuthenga isinkwa
Masihambisane (let us go together)
MANDLA:   Kulungile.

**Answer to sketch:** The Friends: Sipho and Mandla

M: Good morning Sipho  S: Good morning Mandla  M: How are you?  S: I am well, how are you?  M: I too am well. How are things at home?  S: At home it's all right but father is ill.  M: I am sorry to hear that. Is he very sick, that is, is he in hospital?  S: No, he is not in hospital, he is taking medicine at home. Where are you going to now, Mandla?  M: I am going to the shop, I want to buy (i.e. make purchases).  S: What do you want to buy at the shop?  M: At home we need bread, we also need tea.  S: I also want to buy (some) bread. Let us go together.  M: All right.

## Exercise No. 5

(a) *Translate into Zulu*

1. Please come in and sit down.  2. What is your name?  3. Do you speak English?  4. Good-morning Dlamini, how are you today?  5. I am well, sir, how are you.  6. I too am well. How goes it at home?  7. It goes well. I request to see Joyce (= please may I see Joyce).  8. I am sorry, she is not here today.  9. Where do you come from? I come from Ndwedwe.  10. I am going, goodbye — Goodbye.

(b) *Translate into English*

1. Sawubona Khumalo, unjani namuhla?  2. Uyasazi isiNgisi na?  3. Ungaphuza itiye noma ikhofi na?  4. Ungubani igama lakho?  5. Hamba kahle Sipho — sala kahle mnumzana.  6. Sobonana kusasa.  7. Dlamini, uvelaphi?  8. Ngivela eMpangeni mnumzana.  9. Ngena phakathi, ngicela uhlale phansi.  10. Ngiyabonga.

## Recapitulation No. 1

A short recapitulation of progress thus far:

| | |
|---|---|
| Concords relating to People: (paras 1 & 2) | Ngi- U- U- Si- Ni- Ba- |
| General Question: (paras 4 & 5) | Add NA at end of statement: Uthanda inyama na? |
| Incomplete Action: (para 3) | Use 'ya' if no word follows the action Siyafunda, Sifunda isiZulu |
| Some Conjunctions: (para 6) | Kodwa (but)   Ngiyasebenza kodwa uTom   uhlala ekhaya |
| | Futhi (and/also)   Babhema ugwayi futhi baphuza utshwala |
| | Ngoba (because)   Uyakhala ngoba ufuna amaswidi |
| | Noma (or)   Ufuna ukusala noma ufuna ukuhamba na? |

27

| | |
|---|---|
| Infinitive (after Want, Like, etc): (para 7) | Uku- built into following verb<br>UJoe uthanda ukubhema |
| Questions, What, Where, Why: (paras 8–10) | Add to verb -ni (what)  -phi (where)  -elani (why)<br>Sifundani? Uhlalaphi? Baphuzelani? |
| Whereabouts: (para 11) | Concord + -phi (no 'ya')  -khona (present)  Akekho/abekho<br>UGeorge uphi? Ukhona  Akekho |
| Commands and Negative: (para 12) | Verb by itself, plus -ni if to more than one<br>Hamba!  Hambani!<br>Don't: Musa uku-  Musani uku- (if more than one)<br>Musa ukubuya!  Musani ukubuya! |
| Instructions/Requests: (paras 13–16) | Ngifuna u . . ./Ngicela u. . . with following verb ending in -e<br>Ngifuna ubuye kusasa/Ngicela ulande iposi |
| Greetings and Farewells: (paras 17–18) | Sawubona (one)  Sanibona (more than one)<br>Hamba/hambani kahle — Sala/salani kahle |

Complete the following sentences:

1. UMary -thanda -phuza itiye (but) uJoyce (likes) ikhofi
2. We George, —— sebenza na? Cha, ngihlala ekhaya.
3. Abantwana —— khala ngoba (they want) amaswidi.
4. Joseph, (don't) shaya inja!
5. Khuzwayo, uhlala — ? Ngihlala eMlazi.
6. Abantu -thenga- esitolo? Bathenga inyama.
7. USamuel — (where) namuhla? — phandle.
8. Abantwana — esikoleni na? Cha, abekho. (Where are they?) Angazi.
9. (Please call) uGumede manje ngoba sifuna — bona yena.
10. Ngifuna (you to bring) imali kusasa.

Replies to above:
1. u uku kodwa uthanda  2. u ya  3. ba ya bafuna  4. musa uku-  5. phi  6. ba ni  7. uphi u  8. bas Baphi?  9.  Ngicela ubize, uku  10. ulethe

# CHAPTER SIX

Go and Go to (destination stated)
Differentiation/Exclusion/Comparison: not
Pronouns: Emphatic, Absolute, Objective

## 19. *Go and go to (destination stated)*

Compare the following sentences:

UJoe uhamba ebusuku    Joe goes (travels) at night
UJoe uya emsebenzini ebusuku    Joe goes to (his) work at night

Sihamba kahle    We travel (go) well
Siya esitolo    We are going to the shop

Abantu bahamba manje    The people are going now
Abantu baya ekhaya    The people are going home

The word 'hamba' is the term to describe movement generally i.e. go, travel, proceed, walk, move. If a destination is indicated, however, the correct verb is YA, which therefore means: go to, travel to, proceed to, etc. followed by the destination.

Do not confuse this 'ya' with the 'ya' needed to complete an incomplete statement e.g. ngiyasebenza (see para 3). The 'ya' now under discussion is an action, a verb of 'motion towards'.

When used with -PHI: The addition of -phi to a verb turns it into a question of where the action is happening, but because in Zulu the -phi is regarded as a *destination* when movement is involved, you must use 'ya' instead of 'hamba' to ask a question Going where?

Uyaphi?    Where are you going? = You go where? (Not uhambaphi)
o    Abantu bayaphi?    Where are the people going?

Note also that this 'ya' is an action, a verb of motion. You will notice the difference between:

o    UGeorge uyaphi?    George he go where? = Where is George going?
     and

---

○ UGeorge uphi? George he where? = Where is George?

In the latter there is no 'motion towards', it is merely a question of George's whereabouts.


## 20. *Differentiation/exclusion/comparison: 'not'*

Look at the following sentences:

I want Joe or Dick    Ngifuna uJoe noma uDick
○ I want Joe, not Dick    Ngifuna uJoe hhayi uDick

Call Joe not Dick    Biza uJoe hhayi uDick
Don't call Dick, call Joe    Musa ukubiza uDick, biza uJoe

I want tea, not coffee    Ngifuna itiye hhayi ikhofi

○ Go tomorrow not today    Hamba kusasa hhayi namuhla
Go tomorrow, don't go today    Hamba kusasa, musa ukuhamba namuhla

The word HHAYI features in all the above and operates in the sense of 'and not, but not' i.e. the idea of differentiation, exclusion or comparison. It is in frequent use and some of its uses are listed below:

1.    Between nouns (personal and others)
      Mary not Joyce    uMary hhayi uJoyce
      bread not meat    isinkwa hhayi inyama
      the cat not the dog    ikati hhayi inja

2.    Between Adjectives
      this not that    lokhu hhayi lokho
      big not small    -khulu hhayi -ncane
      two not three    -bili hhayi -thathu

3.    Between Adverbs
      outside not inside    phandle hhayi phakathi
      here not there    lapha hhayi lapho
      this morning not this afternoon    ekuseni hhayi ntambama

4.    Between Infinitives
      to walk not (to) run    ukuhamba hhayi ukugijima
      to work not play    ukusebenza hhayi ukudlala

Whereas it is usual to express the comparison by using both ideas with 'hhayi' in between, one idea can be implied e.g.
○ Hhayi manje!   Not now! (meaning: later, not now)
○ Hhayi wena!   Not you! (meaning: someone else, not you)
      Certain expressions embodying 'hhayi' are in frequent use, such as:
      Hhayi khona! (From Fanakalo)   Not so, never, not on your life, etc.
      Hhayi-ke   Well then, very well
○ Hhayibo!   No, I say! Stop it!
      Hhayi!   by itself, or repeated   No, no, no!

30

Special Note: 'Hhayi' cannot be used to described a negative *action* such as: Tom is not working, We don't want to go, It is not raining, etc. nor a negative command, which is 'musa uku-'.

The manner in which negative actions are expressed is set out later in para 40.

You certainly cannot say, for example, 'hhayi funa' (as in Fanakalo) to mean 'not want'.

## 21. *Emphatic pronouns (also known as absolute pronouns)*

The words **Mina, Wena, Yena** and **Thina** feature prominently in Fanakalo, where they are often used as commencing an action i.e. as the subject of a sentence e.g. Mina funa (I want). This is totally wrong, as they should never be used in the place of the personal concords ngi- u- u- si- ni- and ba- but they can be used to *support* them for emphasis or contrast. They can also be used as the object (see para. 22 overleaf).

The words in question are as follows:

| Personal Concord | | Emphatic Pronoun | Meaning |
|---|---|---|---|
| ngi- | I | Mina | I myself, I, as for me |
| u- | You | Wena | You yourself, You, as for you |
| u- | He/she | Yena | He himself/she herself, He/she, as for him/her |
| si- | We | Thina | We ourselves, we, as for us |
| ni- | You (pl) | Nina | You yourselves, you, as for you |
| ba- | They | Bona | They themselves, they, as for them |

By using these words together with the personal concord you give emphasis to the statement, or bring in the following meanings: as for ... as regards ... with regard to ...

*Examples:*

○ *I* work in the day, but *Joe* works at night (as for Joe, he works at night)
Ngisebenza emini mina kodwa uJoe usebenza ebusuku yena (or usebenza yena ebusuku)
They drink beer but *we* drink tea
Baphuza utshwala kodwa siphuza thina itiye

It is common to use these words to commence the action, i.e. before the personal pronoun, e.g.

○ They drink beer but *we* drink tea
Baphuza utshwala kodwa *thina* siphuza itiye
*I* want to go, not you
*Mina* ngifuna ukuhamba, hhayi wena

but the beginner is advised not to do this unless sure of the correct usage (i.e. together with the personal concord), otherwise it is easy to fall into the Fanakalo way of leaving out the personal concord altogether.

In the Command form, the emphatics Wena and Nina are equivalent to 'You there' e.g.

Wozani lapha nina madoda

Come here you men

Shesha wena!

Get a move on, you there!


## 22. As the object

The Emphatic Pronouns listed above can always be used as the object, i.e. after the action. When thus used, their meanings are:

| Subject | | Object | |
|---------|---------|--------|---------|
| ngi | I | mina | me, me myself |
| u- | You | wena | you, you yourself |
| u- | He/she | yena | him/her, him himself/her herself |
| si- | We | thina | us, us ourselves |
| ni- | You (pl) | nina | you, you yourselves |
| ba- | They | bona | them, them themselves |

*Examples:*

○   They want to see us tomorrow
    Bafuna ukubona thina kusasa

○   Where is Joe? I want him now
    UJoe uphi? Ngifuna yena manje

Teacher likes me, not you

Uthisha uthanda mina, hhayi wena

In some situations the use of these Emphatic Pronouns sounds very much like Fanakalo, which has no other way to express the object, whereas Zulu has another way (this, however, is not dealt with in this course).

Note: But see item 5 App II where the alternative is briefly discussed.


## Exercise No. 6

(a)   *Translate into Zulu:*
1. The children like to go to school.   2. John is going now.   3. Please go to the bank and get money.   4. The child walks well.   5. The boys want to run, not walk.   6. Please put the book here not on the table.   7. Joseph studies well at school, but as for you, you play the fool (ganga).   8. Where is Tom? He helps me a lot.   9. The teacher likes to hit us.   10. Father wants to give Tom some money because he likes him a lot.

(b) *Translate into English:*
1. Ngithanda ukuhamba emini hhayi ebusuku. 2. Abantwana baya esikoleni. 3. Ngiyahamba, sala kahle. 4. Abantu baya esitolo ngoba bafuna ukuthenga. 5. Hamba manje, musa ukubuya. 6. Ngithanda itiye hhayi ikhofi. 7. USipho ubhema kakhulu kodwa mina ngibhema kancane. 8. Ubaba ubiza wena. 9. Hhayibo! Musa ukushaya umntwana. 10. Hhayike, hamba manje ubuye kusasa.

*Funda Indaba, Bese Uphendula Imibuzo*
(Phendula Imibuzo = Answer the Questions)
1. Ubaba uyahamba. Uyaphi? Uya esitolo. Ufunani esitolo? Ufuna ukuthenga. Ufuna ukuthengani? Ufuna ukuthenga ugwayi, futhi ufuna iphepha. Usebenzaphi ubaba? Usebenza efektri (in a factory) eThekwini. We George, usebenzaphi wena? Ngisebenza esibhedlela mina. Nihlalaphi? Sihlala eMbumbulu thina. Nivuka ekuseni na? Yebo, sivuka ekuseni kakhulu ngoba sihlala kude (far away).
2. We bantwana, niyaphi? Siya esikoleni. Nikhalelani? Siyakhala ngoba uthisha uthanda ukushaya thina. Niyaganga yini (or what?) esikoleni na? Cha, sifunda kahle. Nifundani? Sifunda isiZulu, futhi sifunda isiNgisi. Nidlala ibhola (soccer) esikoleni na? Yebo, siyadlala, kodwa hhayi amantombazana (the girls).
3. Woza lapha wena, musa ukubaleka. Ungubani igama lakho? Ngingu Joseph Madlala. Uyaphi? Ngiya emsebenzini kodwa ngifuna ukubona umfowethu uDick, ukhona na? Cha, akekho namuhla. Uphi yena? Angazi, mhlawumbe uyagula. Kulungile, ngiyahamba. Sala kahle. Yebo, hamba kahle.

*Imibuzo*
1. Uyaphi ubaba? Ufuna ukuthengani esitolo? Usebenzaphi ubaba, futhi usebenzaphi uGeorge? Bavukelani ekuseni?
2. Abantwana bakhalelani? Bafunda kahle noma bayaganga na? Bafundani esikoleni?
3. UJoseph Madlala uyaphi? UDick ukhona namuhla na? UDick uyagula yini?

# CHAPTER SEVEN

Days and Times
Tenses: Future and Past (recent and remote)
Questions in Future and Past tenses

## 23. Days and times

In this Chapter we will deal with the Future and Past tenses and in order to use them the following vocabulary must now be learnt:

namuhla/namhlanje   today
kusasa   tomorrow
izolo   yesterday
ekuseni   morning, early
ntambama   afternoon
ebusuku   night
emini   during the day, midday
kusihlwa   evening
kuthangi   day before yesterday
ekupheleni kwenyanga   at the end of the month
manje   now
khona manje   right now
masinyane   soon
kade   long ago

*Combining Days and Times*
namuhla ekuseni   this morning
namuhla ntambama   this afternoon
namuhla ebusuku   tonight
kusasa ekuseni   tomorrow morning
kusasa ntambama   tomorrow afternoon
kusasa ebusuku   tomorrow night
izolo ekuseni   yesterday morning
izolo ntambama   yesterday afternoon
izolo ebusuku   last night

---

**Key to Symbols in text** to be used in conjunction with tapes:
  ○   The word or sentence
  ▷   The complete line
  ▶   The complete section

## Specific Times

(always preceded by 'ngo' meaning 'at'. Use English numeral throughout).

ngo-seven    at 7 o'clock
ngo-pasi-six    at half-past six
ngo-ten pasi-two    at ten past two
ngo-kwota pasi-one    at quarter past one
ngo-five thu-ten    at five to ten
ngo-twenty pasi-four    at twenty past four

## Specific Periods

When expressing week, month or year it is usual to imply 'during' and these words are therefore preceded by nga- nge- or ngo- (meaning 'during'). In para 33 it will be explained why these differ.

○  isonto    week
○  ngalelisonto    this week
○  ngesonto elizayo    next week
○  ngesonto eledlule    last week
   inyanga    month
   ngalenyanga    this month
   ngenyanga ezayo    next month
   ngenyanga edlule    last month
   unyaka    year
   ngalonyaka    this year
   ngonyaka ozayo    next year
   ngonyaka odlule    last year

## Days of the Week

Apart from Sunday, these present a difficulty to most students and need to be learnt and practised. The days are named according to activities associated with them, or by number, as follows:

| | | |
|---|---|---|
| Sunday | Isonto | the church day (from Afrikaans Sondag) |
| | | Isonto also means a church or a week (the period between church days) |
| Monday | uMsombuluko | the day of unfolding the week, from sombuluka = become unrolled |
| Tuesday | uLwesibili | the second day, from -bili (two) |
| Wednesday | uLwesithathu | the third day, from -thathu (three) |
| Thursday | uLwesine | the fourth day, from -ne (four) |
| Friday | uLwesihlanu | the fifth day, from -hlanu (five) |
| Saturday | uMgqibelo | the day of completion/covering up, from gqibela = cover up |

It is usual to prefix the word 'on' i.e. Monday in Zulu is usually 'on Monday'. This is built in to the word for the day in question and is always 'ngo-' except for Sunday, which is 'nge-'.

○  On Sunday    ngeSonto
○  On Monday    ngoMsombuluko
○  On Tuesday    ngoLwesibili
○  On Wednesday    ngoLwesithathu

- On Thursday    ngoLwesine
- On Friday    ngoLwesihlanu
- On Saturday    ngoMgqibelo

*Examples of Days and Times:*
- 1.  We start work at 7.30 a.m. and knock off (shayisa) at 5 p.m.
      Siqala umsebenzi ngo-pasi seven ekuseni sishayise ngo-five ntambama.
- 2.  Joe wants to go home at the end of the month.
      UJoe ufuna ukuya ekhaya ekupheleni kwenyanga.
- 3.  I want you (to) return tomorrow afternoon.
      Ngifuna ubuye kusasa ntambama.
- 4.  Mary is staying at home this week because she is ill.
      UMary uhlala ekhaya ngalelisonto ngoba uyagula.
- 5.  We go to town on Saturday.
      Siya edolobheni ngoMgqibelo.

## 24. *Future tense*

Study the following sentences:

We see the children    Sibona abantwana
We will see the children    Sizobona abantwana

George is going now   UGeorge uhamba manje
George will go now    UGeorge uzohamba manje

The children are getting sweets    Abantwana bathola amaswidi
The children will get sweets    Abantwana bazothola amaswidi

I am working    Ngiyasebenza
I will work    Ngizosebenza

He is happy because he is eating    Uyajabula ngoba uyadla
He will be happy because he will eat    Uzojabula ngoba uzodla

It will be seen that:
(a)  The future tense is formed by placing -ZO- between the personal concord and the verb.
(b)  The 'ya' which is used to complete a statement in the present tense (see para 3) is not used in the future tense (it applies to the present tense only).

*Examples* (using days and times):
- 1.  Joe will return next week
      UJoe uzobuya ngesonto elizayo
- 2.  We will shop in town this morning and will return at 3 p.m.
      Sizothenga edolobheni namuhla ekuseni sizobuya ngo-3 ntambama
- 3.  Will you see Tom tonight?
      Uzobona uTom namuhla ebusuku na?
- 4.  Dick will start (to) work on Thursday
      UDick uzoqala ukusebenza ngoLwesine
- 5.  The doctor will come on Monday at nine
      Udokotela uzofika ngoMsombuluko ngo 9

## 25. Past tense (recent)

We will deal firstly with the recent past tense, i.e. from the present up to 3 days ago.

Compare the following sentences:

I am helping father    Ngisiza ubaba
I have helped father    Ngisize ubaba

We are buying bread    Sithenga isinkwa
We have bought bread    Sithenge isinkwa

Joe is coming back    UJoe uyabuya
Joe has come back    UJoe ubuyile

Are they going?    Bayahamba na?
Have they gone?    Bahambile na?

The following observations arise:

(a) The recent past tense is formed by changing the final vowel of the verb to -E if a word follows, and to -ILE if no word follows (remember that the interrogative 'na' is not regarded as a word).

(b) As is the case with the future tense, the 'ya' which is used to complete a statement in the present tense is not used in the past tense.

(c) This tense is used for any action up to 3 days ago, no matter how recent.

e.g.
○    Joe has come    UJoe ufikile
     Joe came just now    UJoe ufike khona manje
○    Joe came this morning    UJoe ufike ekuseni
     Joe came yesterday    UJoe ufike izolo

*Examples* (using days and times):
○    1.    The people finished the work at 11 o'clock
          Abantu baqede umsebenzi ngo 11.
     2.    Are the children at school? Yes, they went at 7 a.m.
          Abantwana basesikoleni na? Yebo, bahambe ngo-7 ekuseni.
     3.    I came very early, I came at 5 a.m.
          Ngifike ekuseni kakhulu, ngifike ngo 5.
     4.    Did you work yesterday? Yes, I did.
          Usebenze izolo na? Yebo, ngisebenzile.

## 26. Past tense (remote)

(Beyond 3 days in the past)
Compare the following:

I see the child today    Ngibona umntwana namuhla
I saw the child yesterday    Ngibone umntwana izolo
I saw the child last week    Ngabona umntwana ngesonto eledlule

Joe is buying a car    UJoe uthenga imoto
Joe has bought a car    UJoe uthenge imoto
Joe bought a car last year    UJoe wathenga imoto ngonyaka odlule

We are learning Zulu    Sifunda isiZulu
o · We learnt Zulu at school    Safunda isiZulu esikoleni

Did you help Sipho yesterday?    Usize uSipho izolo na?
Did you help Sipho last month?    Wasiza uSipho ngenyanga edlule na?

The following points emerge:
(a) Unlike the other tenses, where the personal concord is unaltered but
    amendments are made to the verb, the remote past tense is formed by
    amending the *concord* and leaving the verb intact.
(b) It is formed by changing the concord to end in -A. The 'i' of ngi-, si- and ni-
    drops away, while u- becomes wa-. The concords are thus:

    ngi - (I)      becomes nga-      si - (we)      becomes sa-
    u - (you)      becomes wa-       ni- (you (pl))  becomes na-
    u - (he/she) becomes wa-         ba - (they)    remains ba-

*Examples* (using days and times):
    1.  Joe returned at the end of the month
        UJoe wabuya ekupheleni kwenyanga
    2.  I went to school (= studied) at Umlazi
        Ngafunda eMlazi
    3.  Did you buy the car last month?
        Wathenga imoto ngenyanga edlule na?
o   4.  Dingaan killed Shaka
        UDingane wabulala uShaka
    5.  We came here on Friday last week
        Safika lapha ngoLwesihlanu ngesonto eledlule

## 27. Questions in future and past tenses

What (-ni)?   Where (-phi)?   Why (-elani)?
In the future and remote past tenses, the addition of the above additives to the
verb (which you amend to indicate the tense involved) presents no problems

e.g.
    What are you buying?    Uthengani?
    What will you buy?    Uzothengani?
    What did you buy? (Remote)    Wathengani?

    Why is he crying?    Ukhalelani?
    Why will he cry?    Uzokhalelani?
    Why did he cry? (Remote)    Wakhalelani?

In the recent past tense, however, you must use the *short* form -E because the additives -ni, -phi and -elani are regarded as 'following words'. Note also that -elani becomes -eleni but only in this tense.

e.g.

What have you bought?  Uthengeni? (*Not uthengileni*)
Where did they work yesterday?  Basebenzephi izolo?
Why have they gone?  Bahambeleni?

## Exercise No. 7

(a) *Translate into Zulu:*
1. I will call you just now.  2. Joe will return on Monday.  3. Will you bring the money tomorrow?  4. They will go at seven and return at 2 p.m.  5. Next week father will buy a car.  6. The children will help in the garden on Saturday.  7. Will the people buy bread or meat?  8. Father will wash the car tomorrow.  9. We will get money this afternoon.  10. My brother will go home at the end of the month.

(b) *Translate into English:*
1. Uzohamba na? Cha, ngizosala.  2. Ubaba uzobuya masinyane.  3. Abantu bazothenga kusasa.  4. Ngizofika ngoLwesine hhayi ngoLwesihlanu.  5. Umntwana uzothenga amaswidi.  6. Sizothola imali ekupheleni kwenyanga.  7. UDlamini uzobuya ngoMsombuluka na?  8. Cha, uzofika ngoLwesibili.  9. Abafana bazodlala ibhola ntambama.  10. Ngizothenga imoto ngenyanga ezayo.

(c) *Translate into Zulu:*
1. Has Tom arrived?  2. Yes, he has come, he came at 8 o'clock.  3. I worked yesterday, not the day before.  4. We saw him this morning in the shop.  5. Have they eaten today?  6. Did they go early?  7. The children went to school today.  8. The people started at seven and finished at five.  9. George spoke a lot last night.  10. The child is crying because Mary has gone away.

(d) *Translate into English:*
1. Ngifike izolo.  2. UJoe uphi? Uhambile.  3. Uhambe ngo 11.  4. Usebenze izolo na? Yebo, ngisebenzile.  5. Abantwana abekho ekhaya, baye esikoleni.  6. UMary ufike ekuseni.  7. Niqedile na?  8. Yebo, siqedile, sifuna ukuhamba.  9. Abantu baphuzile na?  10. Yebo, baphuze itiye ngo 10.

(e) *Translate into Zulu:*
1. I went to school (= I studied) at Ndwedwe.  2. Last year I stayed at home.  3. The people planted (tshala) potatoes last year.  4. Did you plant last month?  5. No, I planted mealies (ummbila) last week.  6. I saw Khoza at the end of the month.  7. We bought a car last week.  8. Did you learn English at school?  9. Yes, I learnt English.  10. Tom grew up (khulela) at Umbumbulu.

(f) *Translate into English:*
1. Ngahamba ngonyaka odlule. 2. Ngabuya ngenyanga edlule. 3. Ngaqala ukusebenza ngesonto eledlule. 4. We Peter, wafundaphi? Ngafunda eMpangeni. 5. Madoda, nathengani ngenyanga edlule? 6. Sathola imali ekupheleni kwenyanga. 7. Ngonyaka odlule umntwana wafunda kahle kodwa ngalonyaka uyaganga. 8. Wakhulelaphi uTom? 9. Wakhulela edolobheni. 10. Ngesonto eledlule ngahlala ekhaya.

(g) *Translate into Zulu:*
1. I am going, I will go, I have gone, I went. 2. They are working today, they will work tomorrow, they worked yesterday, they worked last month. 3. Joe will come tomorrow, not on Thursday. 4. I told Gumede this morning and I will tell Khumalo tonight. 5. Last week we brought meat, this week we are bringing bread, next week we will bring tea. 6. I saw Dlamini at home last month. 7. Will you go now? 8. No, I will go this afternoon at 3. 9. Men, have you finished? 10. No, we will finish at 5 o'clock.

(h) *Translate into English:*
1. Ngenyanga ezayo ngizofuna umsebenzi eThekwini. 2. Ngonyaka odlule ngathenga imoto. 3. Abafana bayajabula ngoba ntambama bazodlala ibhola. 4. UDick ubuyile na? Cha, uzobuya ebusuku. 5. UMary uthenge edolobheni ekuseni, uzobuyela ekhaya ntambama. 6. Sizoqeda umsebenzi ngo-5. 7. UJacob uzovakashela (visit) uDoris esibhedlela ntambama. 8. Udokotela wafika ekupheleni kwenyanga, uzofika futhi kusasa. 9. Ngenyanga edlule ubaba waphumula (rest) ekhaya, ngenyanga ezayo uzobuyela (return to) emsebenzini. 10. We Dick, uyahlala yini? Cha, ngizohamba masinyane.

(i) *Translate into Zulu:*
1. You boys, where did you play yesterday? Where did you play last week? 2. What have the children bought at the shop? 3. Why did the child cry during the night? 4. Where did you work yesterday? 5. What are they learning today and what did they learn yesterday? 6. Have you eaten? If so (uma kunjalo) what did you eat? 7. Why did you stay at home last month? 8. Where did you learn to speak English? I learnt at school. 9. Where have the people gone? They went to the shop, they are buying bread. 10. What will you bring tomorrow?

(j) *Translate into English:*
1. We Khoza, uyephi ekuseni? Ngiye esitolo. 2. Uthengeni? Ngithenge ugwayi. 3. Uthengeleni ugwayi, hhayi isinkwa? Ngoba ngiyabhema. 4. Ngonyaka odlule wafundaphi? 5. Udlephi namuhla? Ngidle ekhaya, futhi ngiphuze itiye emsebenzini. 6. Abantwana bazothengani ethilomu? Bazothenga amaswidi. 7. Uzoyaphi kusasa? Ngizoya edolobheni. 8. Wahlalaphi ngenyanga edlule? Ngahlala ekhaya. 9. UTom wakhulelaphi? Wakhulela kwaZulu. 10. UJoyce uyeleni esibhedlela? Ngoba uyagula.

# CHAPTER EIGHT

## Question: When?
## The weather

Learn the following vocabulary:

shisa    be hot
balela    be fine with heat
phola    be cool
baneka    be lightning
imvula    rain (noun)
-makhaza    cold
banda    be cold
-na    to rain (verb)
duma    to thunder (verb)
vunguza    blow strongly (wind)
umoya    wind
sithibele    be overcast
Linjani izulu?    What's the weather like?
Izulu lihle    The weather is fine
Izulu libi    The weather is bad
-thi    to say, think (be of opinion)
ngithi    I think
uthi    you think/he thinks
kunjalo    it is so
akunjalo    it is not so

## 28. Question: When?

To express *when?* we use NINI which is not joined to the verb (like -ni -phi and -elani) but is a word on its own. It can come at the end of the sentence but it is usually more appropriate to place it just after the action being queried. This word is a *question,* relating to a time or period, and must not be confused with the conditional 'when' (e.g. call me *when* he comes) which will be learnt later.

---

Key to Symbols in text to be used in conjunction with tapes:
    ○    The word or sentence
    ▷    The complete line
    ▶    The complete section

*Examples:*

When do they get paid?    Bahola nini?

o    When does she drink tea?    Uphuza nini itiye?    or    Uphuza itiye nini?

When will Tom return?    UTom uzobuya nini?

o    When did Tom return?    UTom ubuye nini?

## 29. *The weather: Izulu*

(Izulu means: the sky, the heavens, the weather)
If you wish to use the indefinite 'it' in Zulu, the word is Ku-

e.g.

it is in order    kulungile
it is pleasant    kumnandi
it's far    kude
it's hot today    kushisa namuhla

When referring to weather conditions, you can use either 'ku-' or 'li-', the latter relating specifically to Izulu (the heavens) or Ilanga (the day).

A few of the more common phrases are set out below:

It is hot    Liyashisa/kuyashisa
It is very hot    Lishisa kakhulu/kushisa kakhulu
It is cold    Kuyabanda/limakhaza
It is fine and warm    Libalele
It is cool    Kupholile
It is thundering/lightening    Liyaduma/liyabaneka
It is overcast    Lisithibele
It is windy    Kunomoya    or    Kuvunguza umoya
It is raining    Liyana    or    Kunemvula
It will rain    Lizona    or    Kuzofika imvula
Perhaps it will rain    Mhlawumbe lizona
Do you think it will rain?    Uthi lizona na?
I think it will rain, what do you think?    Ngithi lizona, uthini wena?
If it rains    Uma lina
If it does not rain    Uma lingani
The weather is nice    Izulu lihle
The weather is bad    Izulu libi

The Weather is always a good topic for conversation. A typical conversation could be on the lines following:

Good-morning Peter. How are you today?
Sawubona Peter, unjani namuhla?

What do you think of the weather (= the weather is how?)

o    Izulu linjani?

It is hot today, not so?
Liyashisa namuhla, akunjalo?

42

But it is windy.
Kodwa kunomoya.

Perhaps it will rain this afternoon or tonight.
Mhlawumbe lizona ntambama noma ebusuku.

What do you think.
Uthini wena?

If it rains tomorrow, I shall stay at home, but if it does not rain I shall go to town.
Uma lina kusasa ngizohlala ekhaya kodwa uma lingani ngizoya edolobheni.

## Exercise No. 8

(a) *Translate into Zulu:*
1. Joseph, when do you start work? 2. When do the children go to school? 3. When will Dick go to Durban? 4. When did Mary arrive? She came this morning at six. 5. They want to go to the shop. When do they want to go? When will they return? 6. Has Tom gone? When did he go? 7. Today it is overcast, I think it will rain 8. Do you say (think) the weather is nice? I myself think it is bad. 9. In Zululand it thunders a lot. 10. If it rains hard the children stay at home.

(b) *Translate into English:*
1. Abantu bahola (draw pay) nini? Bahola ntambama ngoLwesihlanu. 2. Abantwana babuya nini esikoleni? Babuya ngo-3 ntambama. 3. Uvuka nini ekuseni? 4. Uqala nini ukusebenza, uqeda nini? 5. UJoe uphi? Uhambile. Uyephi? Uye esitolo. Ufunani esitolo? Ufuna ugwayi. Uzobuya nini? Uzobuya masinyane. 6. Izulu lihle namuhla ngoba libalele. 7. Lisithibele namuhla, futhi kunomoya. 8. Uthi lizona na? 9. Angazi, mhlawumbe kuzofika imvula ntambama. 10. Uma lina siyeka ukusebenza phandle, singena endlini.

# CHAPTER NINE

And, with: Na-; By means of: Nga-
Fusion with Na- and Nga-
Question: How? (by what means?)


## 30. And: na- plus fusion

Study the following phrases, all of which embody na- (meaning *and*):
here and there    lapha nalapho
inside and outside    phakathi naphandle
bread and meat (inyama)    isinkwa nenyama
bread and jam (ujamu)    isinkwa nojamu
bread and water (amanzi)    isinkwa namanzi
boys and girls    abafana namantombazana
Sipho and Mandla    uSipho noMandla
Joseph and Mary    uJoseph noMary

The following points emerge:
(a)  In paragraph 6 we discussed the use of the conjunction 'and' (Futhi) to join sentences. To join things, persons, names etc. we use the particle 'na-'.
(b)  It is not a separate word but is incorporated into the word following.
(c)  If the word following does not commence in a vowel, na- is simply added in front to form one word.
(d)  If the word following begins with the vowel i- u- or a-, the incorporation of na- creates a new sound, because in Zulu two vowels cannot follow each other in one word without some modification taking place, and one of these modifications is the fusion of the two vowels to give a new sound (in most textbooks this is called Coalescence).
(e)  Nouns and names in Zulu (with a very few exceptions) commence in i- u- or a-. When you use the particle 'na-' in front of any of these, the 'a' of 'na' fuses with the i- u- or a- of the noun following it. Both the 'a' and the following vowel drop away, as they create a new sound, as follows:
a- followed by i- becomes e-
a- followed by u- becomes o-
a- followed by a- remains a-

---

Key to Symbols in text to be used in conjunction with tapes:
  ○    The word or sentence
  ▷    The complete line
  ►    The complete section

44

(f)  This fusion of the vowel 'a' with i- u- or another a- is a common feature of
     Zulu. Other particles, of which a few are: nga- wa- ya- sa- la- etc. are in
     frequent use, being incorporated into following nouns, and the 'a-' of such
     particles follow the same rules of Fusion. They must therefore be well
     learnt and understood. Shortly stated, the rules are:
     a + i = e   a + u = o   a + a = a
(g)  This particle 'na-' means 'and' and does not stand alone. Do not confuse it
     with the general question na (which comes at the end of a sentence) or the
     verb -na meaning 'to rain'.

*Examples:*

○  We see the cat and the dog
   Sibona ikati nenja
   (na + inja)

○  They are eating meat and beans
   Badla inyama nobhontshisi
   (na + ubhontshisi)

   He likes sweets and cakes
   Uthanda amaswidi namakhekhe
   (na + amakhekhe)

   I will buy bread, sugar, milk, butter and potatoes
   Ngizothenga isinkwa noshukela nobisi nebhotela namazambane
   (na + ushukela)   (na + ubisi)   (na + ibhotela)   (na + amazambane)

○  Call Dick, Joe and Gumede
   Biza uDick noJoe noGumede
   (na + uJoe)   (na + uGumede)

   The last example above will show that to join *people's* names, you simply use
   'no-' because all proper nouns start with u-.


## 31. With (after verbs of action): na- plus fusion

Besides meaning 'and', the particle 'na-' is used to indicate 'with' after an
action e.g. go with, work with, play with, talk with, etc.

*Examples:*
   hamba na-   go with, accompany
○  I will go with the child
   Ngizohamba nomntwana

   buya na-   return with = bring back
   They are going to the shop, they will return with tea, bread and sugar
   Baya esitolo bazobuya netiye nesinkwa noshukela

   dlala na-   play with
   The child is playing with a snake
   Umntwana udlala nenyoka

45

hlala na-   stay with
We stay with father at Umlazi
Sihlala nobaba eMlazi

khuluma na-   talk *to (like the Americans and Afrikaners, they say 'talk with')*
○   Joe likes to talk to the girl
UJoe uthanda ukukhuluma nentombazana
You talk with whom = who are you talking to?
Ukhuluma nobani? (ubani = who)

## 32. *And/with: na- when no fusion occurs*

(a) Some examples of na- being joined to the following word without fusion (because there is no second vowel involved) are:
today and tomorrow   namuhla nakusasa
here and there   lapha nalapho
this morning and this afternoon   ekuseni nantambama
○   on Fridays and Saturdays   ngoLwesihlanu nangoMgqibelo
and what? (= what else?)   na- + ni? = nani?

The word 'futhi' is often used in the above, e.g.
○   They are buying bread, and what else?
Bathenga isinkwa nani?
or
Bathenga isinkwa nani futhi?

(b) With Personal endings (me, you etc.):
When you wish to say: and/with me, and/with you, etc. there is no fusion, the particle 'na-' being used with the following endings (which are in fact shortened forms of the Emphatic Pronouns mina, wena, etc. quoted in paragraph 21):

-mi   I, me      -we   you      -ye   he/him, she/her
-thi   We, us    -ni   you (pl)   -bo   they, them

*Examples:*
Go with him   Hamba naye
Joe works with me   UJoe usebenza nami
○   I want to talk to you   Ngifuna ukukhuluma nawe (or nani- plural)

(c) Besides being used directly with a verb, as in above examples, the words nami, nawe, etc. also have the meaning: also, in addition, as well, etc. as detailed below:
nami   and I, I also, I too, me as well, and me, me too, etc.
nawe   and you, you also, you too, you as well, etc.
naye   and he/she, he/she also, he/she too, he/she as well, and him/her etc.
nathi   we also, and we, we too, we as well, and us, us too, etc.
nani   and you (pl), you also, you too, you as well, etc.
nabo   and they, they also, they too, they as well, them too, and them, etc.

These words are used with the personal concord, which they usually precede in the sentence.

*Examples:*

Joe smokes a lot and so do you (= and you too/you also smoke a lot)
UJoe ubhema kakhulu nawe ubhema kakhulu

They stay at Umlazi and so do we (= we also stay at Umlazi)
Bahlala eMlazi nathi sihlala eMlazi

○   Tom is looking for work and so am I (= I too)
UTom ufuna umsebenzi nami ngifuna umsebenzi

The word 'futhi' (= also, too) is often used in these instances, in which case the action need not be repeated e.g. the last example could read:
○   UTom ufuna umsebenzi nami futhi.

As these words can be used for purposes of emphasis, they have a similar function to the Emphatic Pronoun (see para. 21) and it is worth remembering that the formation of both sets of words is similar, except that the syllables are transposed, i.e., nami instead of mina, nawe instead of wena, etc.

## 33. *By means of, with: nga- plus fusion*

If you compare the following phrases:
with a stick (induku)   ngenduku   (by means of)
with a knife (umese)   ngomese   (by means of)
with water (amanzi)   ngamanzi   (by means of)
by bus (ibhasi)   ngebhasi   (by means of)
on foot (izinyawo)   ngezinyawo   (by means of)
you will note that NGA- has the same features as NA- i.e. being built into the following word, with Fusion operating. Nga- has many meanings but in this course we will confine its use to the following:
(a)   *Means of travel*
Learn the following words:
► bus  ibhasi                          taxi  itekisi
   motor cycle  isithuthuthu      feet  izinyawo
   aeroplane  ibhanoyi            car  imoto
   train  isitimela                     bicycle  ibhayisikili

*Examples:*

○   We travel by bus
Sihamba ngebhasi (nga- + ibhasi)

Joe goes to work by car
UJoe uya emsebenzini ngemoto (nga- + imoto)

○   The children go to school on foot
Abantwana baya esikoleni ngezinyawo (nga- + izinyawo)
(To travel on foot is also: hamba phansi (= go on the bottom))
(b)   *Agents*
In English, to indicate the means of performing an action, we say 'with' but we really mean: by means of. In Zulu this is nga-.

47

Learn the following vocabulary of useful words:

| | | | |
|---|---|---|---|
| knife | umese | wire | ucingo |
| axe | imbazo | machine | umshini |
| stick | induku | spear | umkhonto |
| hand | isandla | spade | ifosholo |
| wheelbarrow | ibhala | rake | ireki |
| string | intambo | stone | itshe |
| hammer | isando | stones | amatshe |

*Examples:*

He hits dogs with a stick
Ushaya izinja ngenduku (nga + induku)

Tie the parcel with string or wire
Bopha impahla ngentambo (nga + intambo) noma ngocingo (nga + ucingo)

We cut grass with a machine
Sisika utshani ngomshini (nga + umshini)

Note re Languages: In English, we say 'in' English/Zulu/Afrikaans, but in Zulu it is expressed as: by means of (nga-) e.g. 'in Zulu' is ngesiZulu (nga + isiZulu).

○ Translate into Zulu = Humusha ngesiZulu
(From now on these words will be used at the head of the set exercises)

(c) *Times and Periods*
(These were mentioned in paragraph 23).
At (a specific time)
    at 5 o'clock   ngo-5 (nga + u5)
    at the time   ngesikhathi (nga + isikhathi)
On (a specific day)
    on Saturday   ngoMgqibelo (nga + uMgqibelo)
    on Sunday   ngeSonto (nga + iSonto)
During (a time period)
    during the year   ngonyaka (nga + unyaka)
    (during) last week   ngesonto eledlule (nga + isonto)
Per (time period)
    per month   ngenyanga (nga + inyanga)
    per day   ngelanga (nga + ilanga) or ngosuku (nga + usuku)

## 34. *Question: How? (by what means?): NGANI*

There is of course no fusion when the question -NI is added on to NGA- to form the word NGANI which means: By means of what = How? (By what means).
*Examples:*
○ How do you travel?   Uhamba ngani?
How is Tom cutting the grass? (by what means?)   UTom usika ngani utshani?
Note that there is another 'How' meaning: In what manner, and this will be dealt with later on.

## Exercise No. 9

(a) *Humusha ngesiZulu:*
1. Joe is buying bread, tea and milk at the shop.  2. The children learn English and Zulu at school.  3. I want Albert, George and Peter.  4. Mary likes tea, with sugar and milk and hot water (amanzi ashisayo).  5. The child plays inside and outside on Saturdays.  6. Please go with the child, he wants to buy sweets.  7. Don't play with a snake.  8. Peter is talking to Mary outside.  9. Do you want to go with me to town this afternoon?  10. The people are outside, the doctor will talk to them just now.  11. Dick works in a factory and so do I.  12. The doctor wants to inject (jova) me and you too.

(b) *Humusha ngesiNgisi:*
1. Abantwana bathanda amakhekhe namaswidi kodwa mina ngithanda inyama nesinkwa.  2. UJoe uthengani ethilumu? Uthenga ugwayi (tobacco). Nani futhi? Uthenga umentshisi (matches).  3. Biza uGumede noCele no Vilakazi.  4. Umama uya esitolo uzobuya nesinkwa noshukela namazambane.  5. We George, ukhuluma nobani phandle?  6. Umama uya edolobheni ngoLwesibili nangoMgqibelo.  7. Ubaba ulungisa indawo engadini ngoba uzotshala imifino (vegetables) lapha nalapha nalapho.  8. Mary, uzohamba nobani edolobheni? Ngizohamba noIda.  9. UJoe ufunda isiNgisi, nami ngifunda isiNgisi nesiZulu.  10. UKhoza uphi? Ngifuna ukukhuluma naye.

(c) *Humusha ngesiZulu:*
1. Dick goes to work by train and so do I but Tom goes by bus.  2. We go to town by bus on Saturdays.  3. On Sunday people go to church (esontweni) by car and on foot.  4. Mary, how do you come to Durban? I travel by bus.  5. How do the children get (= travel) to school? They walk (= go on foot).  6. The teacher likes to hit us, he hits with the hand.  7. Dingane killed Shaka with a spear.  8. Do you get paid (hola) by the month? No, I am paid by the week.  9. The child works in a garden in town on Saturday, he gets paid by the day.  10. Last month Joe earned a lot because he worked at night and in the afternoons.

(d) *Humusha ngesiNgisi:*
1. Umfowethu uhamba ngemoto kodwa mina ngihamba ngesithuthuthu.  2. Ufike ngani lapha? Ngifike ngebhayisikili.  3. Ufike nini? Ngifike ngo 3.  4. Umuntu usika umuthi (tree) ngembazo.  5. Abantwana bashaya inja ngamatshe.  6. Ngizobopha impahla ngentambo.  7. UJoe ushaya insimbi (metal) ngesando.  8. Nihola ngani? Ngihola ngenyanga kodwa umfowethu uhola ngesonto.  9. Uhola nini yena? Uhola ngoLwesihlanu ngo 4 ntambama.  10. Abantu baya edolobheni ngesitimela. Bazobuya ngani? Bazobuya ngebhasi.

Now learn the following vocabulary which will be used in the stories that follow: (Translations are in the Answers to Exercises.)

Wenzani?   What do you do, what are you doing?
Wenzeni?   What did you do?

Kuhle   It is good
Kuhle uku . . .   It is good to . . .

Phumula   Rest (verb)
Esitolo   At/in/to the shop
Ezitolo   At/in/to the shops

Vama uku . . .   Be used to, be in the habit of

Umzali   Parent
Abazali   Parents

Impelasonto   The weekend
Abantu abanye   Some people, other people
Abantu abaningi   Many people
Abanye   Some, others (referring to people, such as abantwana, abafana etc.)

Ngesinye isikhathi   Sometimes, at other times
Zonke izinsuku   Every day (= always) (often contracted to zonkinsuku)
Njalo   Always, continually

(e) Funda Indaba:
## NGEMPELASONTO
Abantu abaningi baphumula ekhaya ngempelasonto. Baqeda ukusebenza ntambama ngoLwesihlanu, babuyela emsebenzini ngoMsombuluko ekuseni. NgoMgqibelo sivama ukuya edolobheni, ngihamba nomama nobaba nomfowethu. Sihamba ngebhasi ngoba sifuna ukufika ekuseni edolobheni. Abantu abaningi nabo bathanda ukuya edolobheni ngoMgqibelo, bafuna ukuthenga ezitolo. Abanye bathenga ukudla (food) abanye bathenga izingubo, abanye bathenga izicathulo (shoes) kodwa mina ngithenga amaswidi namakhekhe. Sibuyela (return to) ekhaya ngo-1, sihamba ngesitimela noma ngetekisi. Ntambama siphumula ekhaya. Abanye bathanda ukushaya ibhola, basebenza abanye engadini noma endlini. Thina bantwana (we children) sisiza abazali. NgeSonto sivama ukuya esontweni, sihamba ngo-9 sibuyela ekhaya ngo-11. Ukuya (to go) esontweni sihamba ngezinyawo ngoba kuseduze (it is nearby). Ntambama ngeSonto abanye bashaya ibhola, abanye bafunda iphepha, abanye bayavakasha (visit). Kuhle kakhulu ukuphumula ngempelasonto.

Phendula nansi imibuzo (answer the questions hereunder):
1.   Siyaphi ngoMgqibelo?
2.   Ngivama ukuhamba nobani?
3.   Sihamba ngani edolobheni?
4.   Sihambelani ngebhasi?
5.   Mina ngithanda ukuthengani ezitolo edolobheni?
6.   NgeSonto siyaphi? Futhi, sihamba ngani?
7.   Kuhle yini (is it) ukuphumula ngempelasonto na?

*Answers*
1. Siya edolobheni ngoMgqibelo.
2. Ngihamba nomama nobaba nomfowethu.
3. Sihamba ngebhasi.
4. Sihamba ngebhasi ngoba sifuna ukufika ekuseni.
5. Ngithanda ukuthenga amaswidi namakhekhe.
6. NgeSonto siya esontweni sihamba ngezinyawo.
7. Yebo, kuhle kakhulu ukuphumula ngempelasonto.

Translated answers:
1. We go to town on Saturdays.
2. I go with mother, father and brother.
3. We go by bus.
4. We go by bus because we want to arrive early.
5. I like to buy sweets and cakes.
6. On Sunday we go to church, we go on foot.
7. Yes, it is very good to rest on the weekend.

▶ (f)  Funda Indaba
SIPHO:  Mama, ngicela ukuya ebholeni (soccer match).
MAMA:   Ukusebenza engadini uqedile na?
SIPHO   Yebo, ngiqedile, woza ubone.
MAMA:   Uzohamba nobani?
SIPHO:  Ngizohamba noJames noMandla.
MAMA:   Nizohamba ngani?
SIPHO:  Sizohamba ngezinyawo ngoba kuseduze. Futhi mama ngicela imali.
MAMA:   Ufunelani imali?
SIPHO:  Sikhokha (pay) imali ukungena ebholeni, futhi ngizothenga ulemonethi noma iCoke ngoba ilanga lishisa kakhulu.
MAMA:   Zonk'insuku ufuna imali! Kulungile. Nizobuya nini?
SIPHO:  Sizobuya ngo-6. Ngiyabonga. Sala kahle mama.
MAMA:   Yebo, hamba kahle Sipho.

Phendula nansi imibuzo ngesiZulu:
1. Where does Sipho want to go?
2. Who will he go with?
3. How will they get there?
4. Is it far to go?
5. Why does Sipho want money?
6. What is the weather like?
7. When will they return?

Answers:
1. USipho ucela ukuya ebholeni.
2. Uzohamba noJames noMandla.
3. Bazohamba ngezinyawo.
4. Cha, kuseduze.
5. Ufuna imali ngoba bakhokha ebholeni, futhi ufuna ulemonethi noma iCoke.
6. Ilanga liyashisa.
7. Bazobuya ngo-6.

# CHAPTER TEN

Locatives (nouns, people and place names)
Question: How?
Some conditions and states

## 35. *Locatives (place of action)*

In English, separate words (prepositions) are used to denote 'to, from, at, in and on', but Zulu does not employ such words. Instead, the place of an action is expressed by amending the noun itself.

Now study the following sentences:

(Isandla)
Esandleni    in the hand
Uphethe (holds) imali esandleni    He holds money in the hand

(Umbhede)
Embhedeni    on the bed
Umntwana ulala embedheni    The child sleeps on the bed

(Isikole)
Esikoleni    to school
Abantwana baya esikoleni    The children go to school

(Amanzi)
Emanzini    in the water
Abafana badlala emanzini    The boys are playing in the water

(Umsebenzi)
Emsebenzini    at work
Baphuza itiye emsebenzini    They drink tea at work

(Imoto)
Emotweni    from the car
Letha izimpahla emotweni    Bring the goods from the car

(Isihlalo)
Esihlalweni    on the chair
Umuntu uphumula esihlalweni    The person rests on the chair

---

**Key to Symbols in text** to be used in conjunction with tapes:
    ○    The word or sentence
    ▷    The complete line
    ►    The complete section

(Izihlalo)
Ezihlalweni    on the chairs
Abantu baphumula ezihlalweni    The people are resting on the chairs

(Isibhedlela)
Esibhedlela    to hospital
UMary uzoya esibhedlela kusasa    Mary will go to hospital tomorrow

(Ikhaya)
Ekhaya    at home
Ubaba uhlala ekhaya    Father stays at home

(Umfundisi)
Kumfundisi    from the minister
Baphuma kumfundisi    They are coming away from the minister

(uKhumalo)
KuKhumalo    to Khumalo
Ngizothumela imali kuKhumalo (thumela = send to)
I will send money to Khumalo

The following points emerge:
1. Except for the last two, which refer to people, all the words have been changed to commence with E-.
2. In addition, most of them end in -eni or -ini.
The foregoing is the method by which most locatives are formed.

The following further points should be noted:
(a) Because a locative can have so many meanings, it is the *verb* you use that gives effect to the meaning desired, e.g.
They are playing in the water    Badlala emanzini
They are entering the water    Bangena emanzini
They are going to the water    Baya emanzini
They are coming out of the water    Baphuma emanzini
They are coming away from the water    Basuka emanzini
They are taking stones from the water    Bakhipha amatshe emanzini

(b) All nouns end in one of the vowels (a, e, i, o, u) and the appropriate endings, to form the locative, are:

Ending in -a or -e : change to -eni
intaba = entabeni (hill)
itshe = etsheni (stone)

Ending in -i : change to -ini
ingadi = engadini (garden)

Ending in -o : change to -weni
indawo = endaweni (place)

Ending in -u : change to -wini
itheku = ethekwini (bay)
(the name for Durban)

53

(c) Some words however form their locative merely with the E- and do not change their ending. They are not many. The most common ones are:

ikhaya    home : locative    ekhaya
isitolo    shop : locative    esitolo
isibhedlela    hospital : locative    esibhedlela
ikhanda    head : locative    ekhanda
ihhovisi    office : locative    ehhovisi
inkantolo    court-house : locative    enkantolo
umnyango    door : locative    emnyango
igalaji    garage : locative    egalaji

(d) There are also a few exceptions to the rules about the ending changes. Common ones are:

indlu    (house) = endlini (not endlwini)
insimu    (field) = ensimini (not ensimwini)
isitofu    (stove) = esitofini (not esitofwini)
Also note that
umuzi    (homestead, kraal) = emzini (not emuzini)
and
umuthi    (tree) = emthini (not emuthini)

(e) The great majority of nouns prefix E- to form the locative, but there are a few which use O-. They are not many and those you would need to know are:

udaka    mud : locative    odakeni
udonga    wall : locative    odongeni
ubisi    milk : locative    obisini
ulwandle    sea : locative    olwandle (but elwandle also used)
ucingo    wire, fence : locative    ocingweni

(d) There are certain other features, involving modification of the last consonant of a word if it is b, m or p, but these fall outside the scope of this course e.g. intambo (string), umlomo (mouth), impuphu (meal). The chief factor is that they form their locative, like most other nouns, by commencing with E- and ending in -eni or -ini.

*Examples of the use of Locatives:*

o    1.  Put the meat on the table (itafula)
        Beka inyama etafuleni
     2.  John has come out of the room (ikamelo)
        UJohn uphume ekamelweni
     3.  Jane is pouring (thela) water into the bucket
        UJane uthela amanzi ebhakedeni
     4.  Mother cooks porridge in the pot (ibhodwe)
        Umama upheka iphalishi ebhodweni
     5.  The people are talking in the bus (ibhasi)
        Abantu bakhuluma ebhasini
o    6.  We killed a snake on the path (indlela)
        Sabulala inyoka endleleni
     7.  Many people go to church (isonto) on Sunday
        Abantu abaningi baya esontweni ngeSonto

8. Tom hit the child in the face (ubuso)
   UTom washaya umntwana ebusweni
9. The children are waiting for (lindela) the teacher at the door (umnyango)
   Abantwana balindela uthisha emnyango
10. Some people carry parcels on the head (ikhanda)
    Abantu abanye bathwala izimpahla ekhanda
11. They are drinking tea in the house (indlu)
    Baphuza itiye endlini
12. Children like to play in mud (udaka)
    Abantwana bathanda ukudlala odakeni

## 36. *Locatives where people are involved*

(a) When dealing with a noun referring to a person and commencing in the singular
with u-, or with a person's name (all names start with u-), there is no E. . .eni/ini
to denote the locative 'to' and 'from'. Instead, KU- is used, both in the singular
and plural.

*Examples:*
>     They are coming back from the person
>     Babuya kumuntu
>     They are coming back from the people
>     Babuya kubantu
>     The child wants to go to mother
>     Umntwana ufuna ukuya kumama
> o   I will go to the doctor tomorrow
>     Ngizoya kudokotela kusasa
>     The nurse is coming from the children
>     Unesi uphuma kubantwana
>     Mary is taking tea to Gumede (take to = yisa)
>     UMary uyisa itiye kuGumede

(b) Note that there are some nouns referring to people which do not begin with u-
and these follow the normal E . . . eni/ini rules, e.g.
>     He is going to the induna    Uya enduneni
>     They get money from the chief (inkosi)    Bathola imali enkosini

(c) When dealing with people, apart from 'to' and 'from', there is another meaning
'at the place of', which is KWA followed by the person's name or designation.

*Examples:*
>     kwaDube    at Dube's place
>     kwamfundisi    at the minister's house
>     kwaJacob    at Jacob's house
>     kwaZulu    at the place of the Zulu i.e. in Zululand
>
> o   They will kill a goat at Khumalo's place tomorrow
>     Bazohlaba imbuzi kwaKhumalo kusasa
>
>     Some people get medicines at the doctor's house, not at hospital
>     Abantu abanye bathola imithi kwadokotela hhayi esibhedlela

## 37. Locatives: place names

(1) *Foreign Names*  Merely prefix E- e.g.
  ePitoli (Pretoria)  eLondon  eFilidi (Vryheid)
    My brother works in Johannesburg
    Umfowethu usebenza eGoli
    (this is another name for Johannesburg, igolide = 'gold').
    I will go to Cape Town next month
    Ngizoya eCape Town ngenyanga ezayo

(2) *Local Names*  Most use the prefix E- e.g.
  eMzumbe  eMlazi  eNtabamhlophe
  eMgungundlovu (Pietermaritzburg)  eMtunzini
  but some use KWA e.g.
  kwaMagwaza  kwaMbonambi
  kwaMashu (at Marshall's place — named after Marshall Campbell)

## 38. Question: How? (in what manner?): KANJANI

In paragraph 34 we dealt with the other 'How' (by what means).

How (in what manner) is expressed by KANJANI? which is made up of ka- (indicating manner) and -njani (of what sort). It usually comes after the action being queried.

*Examples:*

o  Abantwana bafunda kanjani esikoleni?
   How are the children getting on (i.e. studying) at school?

o  UTom ushayela (drive) kanjani imoto?
   How does Tom drive (a car)?

   UMary usebenza kanjani?
   How does Mary work?

   The usual answers are:  kahle (well) or kabi (badly)

   UPeter ufunda kahle esikoleni noma ufunda kanjani?
   Does Peter study well at school or what (= how does he study?)

   Ngesinye isikhathi ufunda kahle, ngesinye isikhathi uyaganga
   Sometimes he learns well, at other times he plays the fool

## 39. A few conditions and states

Learn the following words, which relate to a state or condition:
hungry  lambile
cross  -thukuthele
tired  -khathele
in a hurry  -jahile
clever  -hlakaniphile

good, suitable    -lungile
injured    -limele
dead    -file
drunk    -dakiwe

They are used with the concord (which incorporates the meaning 'to be') e.g.
I am hungry = I hungry = Ngilambile
The children are good = children they good = Abantwana balungile
○ Tom is in a hurry = Tom he in a hurry = UTom ujahile

Learn the following vocabulary:
○  put  beka
○  put in  faka
   purse  isikhwama
   cupboard  ikhabethe
   cup  inkomishi
   soil  inhlabathi
   sand  isihlabathi
   races (horse)  umjaho
   fall  wa
   there is  kukhona
   pocket  iphakethe

bottle  ibhodlela
fire  umlilo
town  idolobha
body  umzimba
○  waste, spend  chitha
○  firstly  kuqala
   white person  umlungu
   dish  isitsha
   river  umfula
   rural areas  amaphandle
   sale (e.g. jumble)  indali

## Exercise No. 10

(a) *Humusha ngesiZulu:*
1. Please take the book out of the cupboard.   2. She is putting the money in the purse.   3. We like to buy clothes at a sale.   4. The child fell down, he is injured on the arm.   5. Some people like to work in town, others like to stay in rural areas.   6. Are you going to work (place of work)? No, I am going to the soccer.   7. Dick spent a lot of money at the races.   8. There is food in the dish.   9. Do you like to work in the house? No, I like working outside in the garden.   10. The people are sitting in the sun today because it is cold.

(b) *Humusha ngesiNgisi:*
1. UKhoza usebenza egalaji edolobheni.   2. UMary usebenza kwaCheckers eBerea eThekwini.   3. Uhlalaphi? Uhlala ehostela kodwa ubuyela ekhaya eMzumbe ngempelasonto.   4. UDick uphi namuhla? Uye enkantolo, uzobuya ntambama.   5. Abanye bathanda ukusebenza ehovisi, abanye bathanda ukusebenza efektri (factory).   6. UDube uzothola iphomende (permit) enkosini ngoba ufuna ukutshala umoba (sugarcane).   7. Abantwana bayajabula ngoba baya olwandle namuhla.   8. Kukhona impukane (fly) obisini ebhakedeni.   9. Ubaba uhlala emzini eMbumbulu.   10. Umnu. Jones wabuya eLondon ngenyanga edlule.

(c) *Humusha ngesiZulu:*
1. I am going to the teacher because you put sand in the cup.   2. They drink a lot at Joseph's place on the weekend.   3. Is he going to the chief? No, he is going to the induna first.   4. My brother worked in Cape Town last year but now he is looking for work in Pietermaritzburg.   5. How does Mary work at the factory? She works well, they like her.   6. How does the child speak? He speaks well in Zulu but badly in English.   7. Father is cross because Tom has gone.   8. The people are very hungry.   9. The child is clever and he studies hard at school.   10. The boys are tired because they have run a lot.

(d) *Humusha ngesiNgisi:*
1. Umntwana ulimele emzimbeni ngoba uwe emthini.   2. Uvelaphi (come from) manje? Ngivela kudokotela.   3. Bazohlaba inkabi (ox) kwaKhoza kusasa.   4. Ngonyaka odlule ngabuya eGoli.   5. Umntwana ubhala (write) kanjani? Ubhala kahle.   6. Ubhala ngani? Ubhala ngepenseli nangepeni (pen).   7. Umfana ulungile ngoba ufunda kahle esikoleni. 8. UDick udakiwe namuhla ngoba uphuze kakhulu izolo.   9. Jane, ngicela uvale ihhovisi manje ngoba ngizohamba ngijahile.   10. Umama uyajabula ngoba abantwana bahlakaniphile.


## Recapitulation No. 2

Second recapitulation of progress since Recapitulation No. 1 (on page 27):

| Go and Go To (para. 19) | Hamba if no destination stated<br>uhamba kahle<br>Ya if destination stated<br>(this includes -phi = where?)<br>Bayaphi?   Baya esikoleni |
|---|---|
| Differentiation (para. 20) | Hhayi between opposites<br>(expressed or implied)<br>namuhla hhayi kusasa<br>hhayi manje! |
| Emphatic Pronouns (para. 21) | Mina, wena, etc. only to support concord<br>never in place thereof<br>Ngisebenza kahle mina, wena uyalova |
| Objective Pronouns<br><br>(para. 22) | Mina, wena, etc. can always be used as an object<br>Biza uJoe, ngifuna yena<br>Basiza thina |
| Times and Days (para. 23) | Always prefixed by ngo-<br>(but nge- for Sunday)<br>ngo-7   ngo-pasi 5   ngoLwesine   ngeSonto |
| Time periods (para. 23) | Prefixed by nge- or ngo-<br>(meaning 'during')<br>ngenyanga, ngesonto eledule, ngonyaka ozayo |

| | |
|---|---|
| Future Tense<br>(para. 24) | -zo- between concord and verb<br>sizobuya kusasa |
| Past Tense (Recent)<br>(para. 25) | -e if another word follows, -ile if not<br>bahambe izolo    uJoe ufikile |
| Past Tense (Remote)<br>(para. 26) | Make concord end in -a<br>ngasebenza eGoli    wafundaphi? |
| What? Where? and Why?<br>in other tenses<br>(para. 27) | Future and Remote Past:<br>Merely add -ni -phi -elani to the verb<br>already put into the tense desired<br>Uzothengani?    Bazohlalaphi?<br>Sizokhalelani?    Wathengani?<br>Wahlalaphi?    Wakhalelani?<br>Recent Past: Verb must be in the -e form,<br>not -ile<br>Uthengeni?    Uhlalephi?    Ukhaleleni? |
| Question: When?<br>(para. 28) | Nini — a separate word<br>Uqala nini ukusebenza?    Bazofika nini? |
| The Weather<br>(para. 29) | Izulu linjani?    Liyashisa/kuyashisa etc. |
| And, With<br>(para. 30–32)<br>  1 Nouns<br><br>  2 Actions<br><br>  3 Personal endings<br><br>  4 No fusion | Na- plus Fusion:<br>$a + i = e$   $a + u = o$   $a + a = a$<br>ikati nenja   itiye noshukela<br>isinkwa namanzi<br>hamba nenduna   ukhuluma nobani<br>buya namazambane<br>usebenza nami   ngikhuluma nawe<br>buya naye<br>Where second word does not start in a vowel<br>phakathi naphandle   namuhla nakusasa |
| By means of<br>(para. 33–34)<br>  1 Vehicles<br>  2 Agents<br>  3 How? | Nga- plus Fusion<br><br>ngebhasi   ngemoto   ngesitimela<br>ngesando   ngomshini   ngamanzi<br>Ngani? (= By what means?)<br>uhamba ngani?   Basika ngani utshani? |
| Locatives: to, from, at, in, on<br>(para. 35–37)<br>  1 Places | E...eni/ini (-eni -ini -weni -wini)<br>a-etafuleni   e-embhedeni   i-emsebenzini<br>o-endaweni   u-ezulwini<br>A few have no -eni/ini ending<br>ekhaya   esitolo   esibhedlela |

|  |  |
|---|---|
| 2  People | Ku- only (no change to end of word)<br>kubaba  kumfana  kubantu<br>kwa- = at the place of<br>kwaZulu  kwaGumede  kwamnumzana |
| 3  Place Names | Foreign: E-<br>ePitoli  eCape Town  eParis<br>Local: E- or Kwa-<br>eMlazi  kwaMashu |
| How? (in what manner?)<br>(para. 38) | Kanjani?<br>Ufunda kanjani esikoleni? |
| Conditions and States<br>(para. 39) | Used with concord<br>ngilambile  badakiwe  uthukuthele |

Complete the following sentences:
1. Ba- (are going) emsebenzini kodwa ngiya (to the shop).
2. Letha inyama (not) isinkwa.
3. Ngifuna ufike namuhla hhayi (tomorrow).
4. Uphi uJames? Ngifuna (him) manje.
5. Ngisebenza kahle kodwa (as for you) uyalova (= loaf).
6. Ubaba (came) izolo, u- (will return) kusasa.
7. UTom ufikile na? Yebo, (he has come), uphandle.
8. (I stayed) ekhaya ngonyaka odlule kodwa manje (I want) umsebenzi.
9. Abantu -phumula ekhaya -Mgqibelo na-Sonto.
10. U- (will go) -phi kusasa? (Where did you go) izolo?
11. Uthenge- esitolo? Ngithenge isinkwa. -ni futhi? Ngithenge futhi ugwayi.
12. UMary uzobuya (when)? Uzobuya ntambama (at 4 o'clock).
13. UJames usebenza (with me) (and with) Dick eThekwini.
14. Ngizohamba na- (you) khona manje. Ufuna ukuhamba (with us) na?
15. UDick uhamba (by train) kodwa mina ngihamba -moto.
16. Khipha imali (from the cupboard).
17. Buyisa imali (to) Gumede.
18. UJames usebenza (how?), kahle noma (badly).
19. Ngicela isinkwa ngoba ngi- (am hungry).
20. Abantwana ba- (good) ngoba bafunda kahle esikoleni

*Answers:*
1. ya esitolo 2. hhayi 3. kusasa 4. yena 5. wena 6. ufike, zobuya 7. ufikile 8. ngahlala ngifuna 9. ba ngo nge 10. zoya, uyephi 11. ni na 12. nini ngo4 13. nami no 14. we nathi 15. ngesitimela nge 16. ekhabetheni 17. ku 18. kanjani kabi 19. lambile 20. lungile

# CHAPTER ELEVEN

Negatives:  Conditions
Verbs (present, future and past tenses)
Infinitive
Whereabouts

## 40. Negatives: general discussion

Examine the following (positive and negatives):

A.  I am hungry   Ngilambile
I am not hungry = not I hungry   Angilambile

We are in a hurry   Sijahile
We are not in a hurry = not we in hurry   Asijahile

They are drunk   Badakiwe
They are not drunk = not they drunk   Abadakiwe

He is good   Ulungile
He is not good = not he good   Akalungile

B.  I work here   Ngisebenza lapha
I do not work here = not I work here   Angisebenzi lapha

They like the child   Bathanda umntwana
They do not like the child = not they like the child   Abathandi umntwana

He stays at Umlazi   Uhlala eMlazi
He does not stay = not he stay at Mlazi   Akahlali eMlazi

We are going   Siyahamba
We are not going = not we go   Asihambi

It will be seen that:

1.  The Zulu negative differs from the English in the position of the word 'not'. In a Zulu negative you *start* with 'not' which is the letter A-. It does not stand separately but is incorporated with the concord.

---

**Key to Symbols in text** to be used in conjunction with tapes:
  ○  The word or sentence
  ▷  The complete line
  ▶  The complete section

2.   All the concords are the same in both positive and negative except 'he/she', which changes from u- to aka- in the negative. The following is a table of negatives and must be well studied:

| Positive | | | Negative | |
|---|---|---|---|---|
| I | ngi- | o | Not I | angi- |
| You | u- | o | Not you | awu-* |
| He/she | u- | o | Not he/she | aka- |
| We | si- | o | Not we | asi- |
| You pl | ni- | o | Not you | ani- |
| They | ba- | o | Not they | aba- |

*Note*: We have now experienced three different uses of 'Not' and this confuses some beginners. The other two are:

Command/Request in the Negative: This is Musa uku-. . . (see para. 15).
Do not go   Musa ukuhamba
Don't speak   Musa ukukhuluma

Differentiation: This is hhayi (see para. 20)
Me, not you   mina, hhayi wena
today, not tomorrow   namuhla, hhayi kusasa
Not now!   hhayi manje!

The 'not' which is now under discussion is the negative of an action (verb) or adjective (condition), i.e.

Action:   They are working   Bayasebenza
They are not working, they don't work   Abasebenzi

Adjective:   They are good (condition)   Balungile
They are not good   Abalungile

He is drunk   Udakiwe
He is not drunk   Akadakiwe

## 41. Negative of an action (verb)

Whereas the negative of an Adjective (condition) merely requires an A- in front, the negative of a verb requires additional amendment, and that is a change in the verb itself. The following are the required changes:

*Present Tense*: Last letter of verb is changed to -i

*Example:*
Ngithanda inyama   I like meat
Angithand*i* inyama   I don't like meat

---

* This appears to be a new word but it is not. If you say 'a' and the 'u' with normal speed, you find that a 'w' forms automatically. I call this a 'cushion'. The only new element in the above table is aka-, the others being merely the normal concord preceded by an a-.

Bayakhuluma    They are talking
Abakhulum*i*    They are not talking
(Note that there is no 'ya' in the negative)

*Future Tense*: -zo- is changed to -zu- (no change at end of verb)

*Example:*
Sizobuya kusasa    We will return tomorrow
Asiz*u*buya kusasa    We will not return tomorrow

*Past Tense* (both Recent and Remote): Verb ends in -anga

*Examples:*
Ngihambe izolo    I went yesterday
Angihamb*anga* izolo    I didn't go yesterday

Bahambile    They have gone
Abahamb*anga*    They have not gone

Wabuya ngonyaka odlule    He returned last year
Akabuy*anga* ngonyaka odlule    He did not return last year

*Further examples:*
Present:
Ngisebenza eThekwini    I work in Durban
o    Angisebenzi eThekwini    I do not work in Durban

Ufunda kahle    You read well
Awufundi kahle    You do not read well

Sifuna uJoe    We want Joe
Asifuni uJoe    We don't want Joe

The children are running    Abantwana bayagijima
o    The children are not running    Abantwana abagijimi

Future:
UMary uzothenga izingubo esitolo    Mary will buy clothes at the shop
o    UMary akazuthenga izingubo esitolo    Mary will not buy clothes at the shop

Abantu bazohamba ngesitimela    The people will travel by train
Abantu abazuhamba ngesitimela    The people will not travel by train

Past:
Sifike ekuseni    We came early
o    Asifikanga ekuseni    We did not come early

Usebenze izolo    You worked yesterday
Awusebenzanga izolo    You did not work yesterday

UTom uhambile ngoba uyagula    Tom went because he is sick
UTom akahambanga ngoba akaguli    Tom didn't go because he is not ill

Umfowethu wathenga imoto    My brother bought a car
o    Umfowethu akathenganga imoto    My brother did not buy a car

A possible aid to remembering the Negative is the well-known 'angazi' = I don't know.

## 42. Negative with infinitive (to . . .)

Study the following:
Ngifuna ukuhamba    I want to go
o    Angifuni ukuhamba    I don't want to go

Abantwana bathanda ukudlala    The children like to play
o    Abantwana abathandi ukudlala    The children do not like to play

Sizozama ukufunda    We will try to learn
Asizuzama ukufunda    We will not try to learn

Abafunanga umsebenzi    They didn't want (look for) work
Abafunanga ukusebenza    They didn't want to work

Asithandi itiye    We do not want tea
Asithandi ukuphuza itiye    We do not want to drink tea

It will be noted that the 'uku-' remains attached to the action desired: it is the main action of wanting, liking, trying etc. which is put into the negative.


## 43. Negative of whereabouts

In paragraph 11 we learnt that 'khona' expresses the presence or whereabouts of a person. This word is however not an *action* and therefore does not experience the changes set out above, to make it negative, but the negative table (angi- awu- aka- asi- ani- aba-) must be used, as in all negatives. The word 'khona' is however shortened to -KHO to indicate the negative and we will deal with the present tense only.

*Examples:*

Ngikhona    I am present
Angikho    I am not present
Angikho phandle    I am not outside

Ukhona    You are present
Awukho    You are not present
Awukho ekhaya    You are not at home

Ukhona    He is present
Akakho/akekho    He is not present
Akekho/akakho ekhaya    He is not at home

Sikhona    We are present
Asikho    We are not present
Asikho ekhaya    We are not at home

Nikhona    You (pl) are present
Anikho    You (pl) are not present
Anikho esitolo    You are not at the shop

64

Bakhona    They are present
Abakho/abekho    They are not present
Abekho/abakho ekhaya    They are not at home

In paragraph 11 we dealt only with akekho/abekho (he/they are not here) but are now able to express the negative for all the personal concords.

Note:  For negative of 'Why?' see item 1 App II

## Exercise No. 11

(a)  *Humusha ngesiZulu:*
1. Are you hungry? No, I am not (hungry).   2. John is not tired but he is very cross.   3. They are not good because they drink a lot.   4. The boys have been fighting (-lwa = fight) but they are not injured.   5. I don't see a dog, I see a cat.   6. The children don't like porridge.   7. You don't talk English very well.   8. They don't go to town on Saturday.   9. I want coffee, not tea; also, I don't want sugar.   10. John doesn't work, he likes to play football not to study.

(b)  *Humusha ngesiNgisi:*
1. Abantwana abahlakaniphile.   2. UJohn akalambile ufuna itiye kuphela (only).   3. UTom uphuze kakhulu izolo kodwa akadakiwe.   4. UJohn uphi? Angazi.   5. Mama, asifuni ukuya esikoleni namuhla.   6. UMary akapheki, ugeza izingubo.   7. Umntwana akafundi isiNgisi esikoleni.   8. Angisebenzi ebusuku, ngisebenza emini kuphela.   9. Abantu abahambi ngesitimela ngeSonto.   10. Ngithanda itiye, angithandi ikhofi.

(c)  *Humusha ngesiZulu:*
1. We will not come tomorrow.   2. They will not bring the money.   3. Joe won't work tomorrow because he is ill.   4. I will not tell you again (futhi).   5. Tom didn't work yesterday and he won't work today.   6. We won't buy bread, we will just buy sweets.   7. Did you see Tom at the shop? No, I did not see him.   8. I did not learn Zulu at school.   9. I will not help you because I am tired.   10. Joe didn't go to work today.

(d)  *Humusha ngesiNgisi:*
1. Asizufika kusasa, mhlawumbe sizofika ngesinye isikhathi.   2. Uzoletha inyama na? Cha, angizuletha inyama, ngizoletha isinkwa kuphela.   3. UMary akazuya edolobheni kusasa ngoba uye edolobheni izolo.   4. Wafunda isiNgisi esikoleni na? Cha, angifundanga isiNgisi, ngafunda isiZulu kuphela.   5. UJames uhambile kodwa akathathanga ukudla (food).   6. Asibonanga inja endleleni.   7. Angifikanga ngo-pasi-8, ngifike ekuseni emsebenzini.   8. Abantwana abazuhleka, bazokhala.   9. uJames ubuyile na? Cha, akabuyanga.   10. Angilalanga ekhaya ebusuku izolo, ngilale emsebenzini.

65

(e) *Humusha ngesiZulu:*
1. The child is not here today.   2. Joe, where are you? I am here outside, I am not in the house.   3. The people have not gone to work today, also they are not at home.   4. Where are they? I don't know.   5. I do not want to play, I want to work.   6. Joe does not like to work at night.   7. We will not try to help the induna.   8. The children will not want to study, they will want to play.   9. You don't like to help people.   10. Joe doesn't like to talk a lot.

(f) *Humusha ngesiNgisi:*
1. UTom akakho emsebenzini namuhla.   2. Abantwana bayephi ngoba abekho esikoleni?   3. Angazi, mhlawumbe baye ebholeni.   4. We James, uphi? Mnumzana, angikho ehhovisi ngilapha phandle.   5. UMary akafuni ukuthenga namuhla.   6. Abantwana abafuni ukugeza ekuseni ngoba kuyabanda.   7. We mntwana, awufuni yini ukufunda namuhla? Cha, thisha, ngiyagula.   8. Asithandi ukuhamba ngezinyawo, sithanda ukuhamba ngemoto.   9. Angizuzama ukuqeda umsebenzi namuhla ngoba sekuhlwile (it is now getting dark), ngizobuya kusasa.   10. Abantwana bathanda ukufunda ngoMgqibelo na? Abanye bayathanda, abanye abathandi.

# CHAPTER TWELVE

If/When (conditional happening)
To think, say, be of opinion
To express a wish, hope, or request

## 44. *If/When (conditional happening): UMA*

Examine the following sentences, where 'uma' (if, when) is used:

○ Siyajabula uma sithola imali
We are glad when we get money
Ngicela ungene phakathi uma ngishaya insimbi
Please come inside when I ring the bell
Kulungile ukuhamba uma uqedile umsebenzi
It is OK to go when you have finished the work
Madoda, hambani uma nibona induna
Men, go when you see the induna
Umntwana ujabula kakhulu uma ebona intombazana
The child is very happy when it sees the girl

○ Abantu baya esitolo uma befuna isinkwa
People go to the shop when they want bread
Abantwana bayadlala uma bethanda
Children play when they like (to)
Uma ngifika ekhaya ngithanda ukuphuza itiye
When I come home I like to drink tea
Uma kufika imvula, abantwana bangena endlini
When the rain comes, the children come into the house

It will be noted that:

1. 'If' and 'When' have different meanings in English, but Zulu uses the one word UMA.
2. It is a conjunction joining independent sentences, therefore you use 'ya' in the first sentence if there is no word following.
3. 'He/she' and 'They' change from u- and ba- to e- and be- after UMA, but all other concords remain the same.

---

4. As in English, you can *start* the sentence with the conditional element if you wish.

5. Phrases such as 'when they want to', 'if you try to', 'if he wishes to' etc. are rendered without the word 'to' in Zulu. In this respect, 'uma' is similar to 'ngoba — because', e.g.

    They play because they want to
    Bayadlala ngoba bathanda
    I ride a bicycle because I like to
    Ngigibela ibhayisikili ngoba ngithanda.

There is another word expressing 'when' which can be used instead of 'uma', and that is: ngesikhathi = at the time that. It is used in the same way as 'uma', with u- and ba- changing to e- and be-, but it usually refers to a sure happening (when, at the time that) as compared with a possible happening (if), e.g.

○ The child cries when I go to town
    Umntwana uyakhala ngesikhathi ngiya edolobheni

○ Children run when they come out of school
    Abantwana bayagijima ngesikhathi bephuma esikoleni
    For negative 'if not' see item 6 Appendix II Page 118

## 45. *Think, say, be of opinion*

There are three words commonly used in above connection:
-Cabanga, -Thi and -Sho

(a) *CABANGA* means 'think'. It is a regular verb, making the usual changes in the negative and the tenses, e.g.

    UJoe ucabanga kakhulu    Joe thinks a lot (i.e. is a thinker)
    UDick akacabangi kahle uma edakiwe    Dick does not think well if he is drunk

If used in the expression 'think that' i.e. be of the opinion, the word UKUTHI (meaning 'that') must be used after 'cabanga', e.g.

○ I think that Joe has gone    Ngicabanga ukuthi uJoe uhambile
    We think that it will rain tomorrow    Sicabanga ukuthi lizona kusasa
    Do you think I like working at night?
    Ucabanga ukuthi ngithanda ukusebenza ebusuku na?

(b) *-THI* means: say, think, be of opinion. It is irregular and the following should be noted:

(1) The actual words of the opinion or action involved must be quoted and not merely a reference or condensed statement, e.g.

    I think the people will come tomorrow
    Ngithi abantu bazofika kusasa
    They think they will get work    Bathi bazothola umsebenzi
    He says he is ill    Uthi uyagula
    We say we do not want to go to work
    Sithi asifuni ukuya emsebenzini

(2) Unlike 'cabanga' the word UKUTHI is never used after 'thi'.

(3) It is often used with -ni (= what?) e.g.

○ Abantu bathini? Bathi balambile
    What do the people say? They say they are hungry.

68

Ngithi lizona ntambama, uthini wena?
I think it will rain this afternoon, what do you think?

(4) The Future is normal (-zothi) and the Recent Past is -the e.g.
Bazothi bayagula    They will say they are ill
Utheni?    What did you say?
Ngithe akasebenzanga kahle izolo
I said he did not work well yesterday

(5) Expressions such as: the time is ... the number is ... can be rendered as:
the time *says* (isikhathi sithi), the number *says* (inombolo ithi), e.g.
What is the time?    Isikhathi sini?
It is 5.30    Sithi pasi 5
The number is 22222    Inombolo ithi 22222

(c) -*SHO* has the same meaning as '-thi' but is not followed by the actual words. It is irregular. For the present, use it mainly with 'njalo' to give the phrase: -sho njalo = think so, say so, e.g.

Ngisho njalo
I say so, that's what I say, that's what I think
Abantu balambile na? Yebo, basho njalo
Are the people hungry? Yes, they say so

For the Negative, e.g. I don't think so, use the Negative Table (angi- awu- aka- etc.) followed by -sho (it is not changed to end in -i).

Akasho njalo
He does not think so
UTom uthi usebenza kahle kodwa mina angisho njalo, ngithi uyalova.
Tom thinks (says) he works well but I do not think so, I think he loafs.

Funda Indaba:
▶ A:  Uphi uTom namuhla?
   B:  Angazi, akafikanga
   A:  UTom uyagula na?
   B:  Abanye bathi uyagula
   A:  Uthini wena? uTom uyagula na?
   B:  Cha, angisho kodwa abanye basho njalo
   A:  Mina ngithi uTom uyaganga, akafuni ukusebenza
   B:  Nami ngisho njalo

*Answer:*
   A:  Where is Tom today?
   B:  I don't know, he has not come.
   A:  Is Tom ill?
   B:  Some say he is ill.
   A:  What do you say? Is Tom ill?
   B:  No, I don't think so but some (others) say so.
   A:  I myself think Tom is fooling, he does not want to work.
   B:  And I think so too.

### 46. To express a wish, hope or request

Learn the following words which apply to above situations:

funa    want, desire
thanda    like, desire, be pleased
cela    request, ask for
themba    hope, expect
fisa    wish, desire
tshela    tell, instruct

A.  If the desired action is to be done by the speaker himself, use 'uku-' meaning: to (i.e. the infinitive, see paragraph 7).

*Examples:*

They wish to learn English
Bafisa ukufunda isiNgisi

o    I request to go home now
Ngicela ukuya ekhaya manje

Joe hopes to find work in Durban
UJoe uthemba ukuthola umsebenzi eThekwini

B.  If the desired action is to be done by another party, the verb of such action must end in -e (in the present tense) and the link word is not uku- but UKUTHI = that, i.e. want *that* you do something, hope *that* we ... Request *that* they ... etc. In some cases 'ukuthi' is dispensed with, being implied, but it is always correct to use ukuthi.

*Examples:*

They want us to go now = They want that we go now
Bafuna ukuthi sihambe manje

Tell the people to return tomorrow = Tell the people that they return tomorrow
Tshela abantu ukuthi babuye kusasa

I request that you help the child
Ngicela ukuthi usize umntwana

Note: The expression 'Please' is in fact 'I request that ...' with the word 'ukuthi' omitted, although it is always permissible to use it, e.g.

o    Please bring the book = I request that you bring the book
Ngicela ukuthi ulethe ibhuku
or
Ngicela ulethe ibhuku

Note: Apart from changing the desired action to end in -e, another feature which is applicable to wishing, desiring, hoping, instructing, etc. is that if the desired action is to be performed by 'he or she', u- is changed to a-, but this is the only case in which the concord undergoes a change.

*Examples:*

They want Joe to talk = They want that Joe (he) talk
Bafuna ukuthi uJoe akhulume

Mary has come, the people request that she sing (cula)
UMary ufikile, abantu bacela ukuthi *a*cule

○ Tell Duma to go now = Tell Duma that he go now
Tshela uDuma ukuthi *a*hambe manje

For another use of Ukuthi see item 7 Appendix II on Page 118

## Exercise No. 12

(a) *Humusha ngesiZulu:*
1. Help the induna if you like.  2. The child cries when it is hungry.  3. I drink tea when I return from town.  4. We play football in the afternoon if we want to (like).  5. We don't like to work outside if it rains.  6. If you are hungry, ask for bread.  7. When the teacher arrives the children keep quiet.  8. Tom drinks a lot on Friday nights when he has been paid (to be paid = hola).  9. If you see Joe at the shop, give him the money.  10. I don't want Gumede here if he is drunk.

(b) *Humusha ngesiNgisi:*
1. Ngifuna ulethe imali uma ufika kusasa.  2. Abantu abathandi ukusebenza uma belambile.  3. Madoda, ngifuna nibuye emsebenzini masinyana uma niholile.  4. Uma lina kusasa asizusebenza phandle.  5. Ngizoya edolobheni uma lingani.  6. Abantwana bathenga amaswidi uma bethanda.  7. Abantu bayajabula ngesikhathi behola (imali).  8. Ngicela ulethe ikhofi ngesikhathi ngingene ehhovisi.  9. Abafana bayagijima ngesikhathi bephuma esikoleni ngoba bafuna ukushaya ibhola.  10.Ngithanda ukuhamba ngezinyawo uma ngiya esontweni ngoba akukude (it is not far).

(c) *Humusha ngesiZulu:*
1. I think the doctor has come.  2. We say we like to work here.  3. The children say they want sweets.  4. If you ask him he will say he is sick.  5. What did they say? They said they want to go home.  6. Do you think Joe will come? Yes, I think so.  7. I do not think they like to work here.  8. Do they say that (so)? Some say so.  9. We request that we go home this afternoon.  10. I like Joe to drive the car because he drives well.  11. Tom wishes to get work next year because he wants money.  12. The boys want me to play football with them.

(d) *Humusha ngesiNgisi:*
1. Umuntu uthi ulambile, futhi ufuna imali.  2. Usho njalo na? Uphumaphi yena?  3. Uthi uphuma ekhaya eNdwedwe.  4. Tshela yena ukuthi angene, ngifuna ukukhuluma naye.  5. Abantwana bathemba ukuthi uthisha uzofika namaswidi esikoleni kusasa.  6. Mnumzane, ngifisa ukukhuluma noAlbert. Ukhona na?  7. Cha, uhambile, uthi uzobuya ntambama.  8. Uyephi? Ngicabanga ukuthi uye kudokotela ngoba uyagula.  9. We Jane, sicela ulethe imali kusasa.  10. Ngesikhathi ungena ehhovisi uzocelani kumnumzana? Ngizocela ukuya ekhaya ekupheleni kwenyanga.

# CHAPTER THIRTEEN

Nouns: general, animal class, people class
Possessives
Question: Whose?
Negatives of nouns

## 47. Nouns: general observations

Study the following sentences:

Umfana uphuza amanzi   The boy drinks water
Abafana baphuza amanzi   The boys drink water

Umuntu uphuza amanzi   The person drinks water
Abantu baphuza amanzi   The people drink water

Inja iphuza amanzi   The dog drinks water
Izinja ziphuza amanzi   The dogs drink water

Isiguli siphuza amanzi   The patient drinks water
Iziguli ziphuza amanzi   The patients drink water

The following are some of the features regarding nouns:
1.  Nouns consist of two elements: a prefix, which is changed to indicate the plural, and a stem, which is constant. Thus in the words quoted above, we have:
umfana
  stem   -fana
  prefix: *Singular*   um-
      *Plural*   aba-
  Complete noun: *Singular*   umfana   a boy
          *Plural*   abafana   boys

umuntu
  stem   -ntu
  prefix: *Singular*   umu-
      *Plural*   aba-
  Complete noun: *Singular*   umuntu   a person
          *Plural*   abantu   people

---

**Key to Symbols in text** to be used in conjunction with tapes:
  ○   The word or sentence
  ▷   The complete line
  ▶   The complete section

72

inja
    stem  -nja
    prefix: *Singular*  i-
             *Plural*  izi-
    Complete noun: *Singular*  inja  dog
                  *Plural*  izinja  dogs
isiguli
    stem  -guli
    prefix: *Singular*  isi-
             *Plural*  izi-
    Complete noun: *Singular*  isiguli  patient
                  *Plural*  iziguli  patients

2. Because the stem is constant, in a Zulu-English dictionary the noun is listed under the stem and not under the first letter of the word, e.g. umfana will be found under Fana (most dictionaries give additional data, e.g. -fana (umfana, aba-) i.e. the prefix and the plural prefix).

3. Every action (verb) must be linked to the noun that performs such action and this link is taken from the prefix of the noun, e.g. umfana has the link 'u' while abafana has the link 'ba': inja has the link 'i' while izinja has the link 'zi': isiguli has the link 'si' while iziguli has the link 'zi'.

4. Because these links come out of the prefix, they carry the same **sound** and are termed CONCORDS accordingly. There is harmony between the prefix and the concord. It must strike you as a discord (the opposite of concord) if you were to say, for instance, inja **u**phuza, because there is no sound of 'u' in the prefix of the word 'inja'. Similarly, it would be wrong to say: izinja **ba**phuza, because there is no 'ba' sound in 'izinja'.

5. Nouns are divided into classes according to their prefixes. There are 8 classes but 3 are not very common. The remaining 5 have the following singular prefixes: um-, umu- (persons): um-, umu (things): ili-, i-: isi-: im-, in-. The concords of the foregoing classes are: u, u, li, si and i. Instead of giving the noun classes a number (which is done in most grammar books) I identify the class by the **sound** of the concord, so that when you come across a noun you do not need to worry about what class it is in, but because you can immediately identify the concord, you can use it straight away.

In this course only two of the noun classes are dealt with, but see item 6 App II for brief reference to three more classes.

6. Concords provide the link not only to the **action** but also to words describing the noun (adjectives), as shown in the following sentences:

My fowls are four, they are small, they are drinking water in the garden
My children are four, they are small, they are drinking water in the garden

In Zulu, putting the noun first, these are rendered as:
Fowls they + my   they + 4   they + small   they + drink water in garden
Children they + my   they + 4   they + small   they + drink water in garden

Izinkukhu zi- + -ami  zi- + -ne  zi- + -ncane  zi- + phuza amanzi engadini
Abantwana ba- + -ami  ba- + -ne  ba- + -ncane  ba- + phuza amanzi engadini

Izinkukhu zami zine zincane ziphuza amanzi engadini
which has a totally different linkage sound from
Abantwana bami bane bancane baphuza amanzi engadini
because 'fowls' and 'children' are in different classes.

7.   Concords cannot stand alone but are built into the words they govern. A common mistake made by beginners is to use a verb without a concord, e.g. the boy works well, which, taking the English literally, would be wrongly given as: umfana sebenza kahle. It should be: Boy he + work well = Umfana *u*sebenza kahle. See also paragraph 2 (d) in this connection.

8.   The great majority of nouns begin with i- or u- (in the singular) and it is important to hear the *beginning* of a word so that you can use the correct concord, e.g.
umngane means : a friend, its concord is u-
ingane means : an infant, its concord is i-


## 48.  *Noun class: I'm In*

This is commonly called the Animal Class, as most of the animals are in it, but there are many other nouns in this class that do not refer to animals, and there are some that refer to people.

Any noun beginning with an I- and followed by M- or N- belongs to the class I have called I'M IN (because of this feature), e.g. imbuzi (goat), imbali (flower), inja (dog), indawo (place).

The plurals are: izimbuzi   izimbali   izinja   izindawo
The concords of this class are: Singular i-   Plural zi-
A list of useful words in this class is set out below:

| | Singular | Meaning | Plural |
|---|---|---|---|
| | imali | money | — |
| | imoto | motorcar | izimoto |
| o | impahla | package | izimpahla |
| | imbali | flower | izimbali |
| | indlovu | elephant | izindlovu |
| | inyoni | bird | izinyoni |
| | inkabi | ox | izinkabi |
| | inyoka | snake | izinyoka |
| | ingulube | pig | izingulube |
| | ingane | infant | izingane |
| | indlu | house | izindlu |
| | ingozi | accident/danger | izingozi |
| | inyanga | month, moon | izinyanga |
| o | incwadi | letter | izincwadi |
| | insimbi | iron, bell | izinsimbi |
| | indawo | place | izindawo |
| | indlela | path | izindlela |
| | induku | stick | izinduku |
| | impuphu | mealiemeal | — |

74

| | | |
|---|---|---|
| imvula | rain | izimvula |
| imvu | sheep | izimvu |
| imbuzi | goat | izimbuzi |
| inyama | meat | izinyama |
| inhlanzi | fish | izinhlanzi |
| inkomo | beast (cattle) | izinkomo |
| inja | dog | izinja |
| inkukhu | fowl | izinkukhu |
| induna | headman | izinduna |
| into | thing | izinto |
| ingubo | item of clothing | izingubo |
| intaba | hill, mountain | izintaba |
| ingadi | garden | izingadi |
| indwangu | cloth | izindwangu |
| ○ indaba | matter, affair | izindaba |
| intambo | string, rope | izintambo |

Exceptions: There are a few nouns in this class that have a normal singular (concord i-) but have ama- in the plural (concord a-). They are not many and refer mainly to people and relationships. Those you would need to know are:

| | | |
|---|---|---|
| inkosi   chief, king | *plural* | amakhosi |
| inkosana   prince, son of the house | *plural* | amakhosana |
| inkosazana   princess, daughter of the house | *plural* | amakhosazana |
| inkosikazi   queen, married woman, madam | *plural* | amakhosikazi |
| indoda   man, husband | *plural* | amadoda |
| indodana   son | *plural* | amadodana |
| indodakazi   daughter | *plural* | amadodakazi |
| intombazana   young girl | *plural* | amantombazana |
| (also, woman in domestic service) | | |

There are also a few nouns that do not conform to the 'I'm in' rules, mainly a few commencing in- but followed by a vowel e.g. inani (price).

*Examples:*
○ The dog is eating meat = dog it + eat meat
    inja i + dla = Inja idla inyama
○ The dogs are eating meat = dogs they + eat meat
    izinja zi + dla = Izinja zidla inyama

The infant is crying = infant it + cry
ingane i + yakhala = Ingane iyakhala
The infants are crying = infants they + cry
izingane zi + yakhala = Izingane ziyakhala

○ The car runs well = car it + run well
    imoto i + hamba kahle = Imoto ihamba kahle
○ The cars run well = cars they + run well
    izimoto zi + hamba = Izimoto zihamba kahle

75

### 49. *Noun class: You People*

(i)   Nouns in this class start with u-, um- or umu- and refer to people.
      The plural is aba- (but there is a small sub-class which does not have this plural
      — see paragraph (v) below).
      The concords are: Singular u-   Plural ba-

(ii)  I have called it the YOU PEOPLE class because if a noun starts with a U- and
      refers to a person, it falls in this class. There are other nouns starting with U-
      which do not refer to people and do not have aba- as the plural.

(iii) Words in this class you would need to know are:

| | | | |
|---|---|---|---|
| umfana | boy | *plural* | abafana |
| umntwana | child | *plural* | abantwana |
| umfowethu | my brother | *plural* | abafowethu |
| umfundisi | parson | *plural* | abafundisi |
| umlungu | White person | *plural* | abelungu (not abalungu) |
| umngane | friend | *plural* | abangane |
| umhlobo | relative | *plural* | abahlobo |
| umuntu | person | *plural* | abantu |

(iv)  Note that in the personal concords with which this course commenced, (ngi- u-
      *u*- si- ni- *ba*-) the u- (he/she) and ba- (they) are in fact the concords of the You
      People class.

*Examples:*

        The boy is playing outside    Umfana udlala phandle
        The boys are playing outside    Abafana badlala phandle
   o    My brother works in Durban    Umfowethu usebenza eThekwini
   o    My brothers work in Durban    Abafowethu basebenza eThekwini

(v)   A few other nouns you need to know fall into a separate section of this class.
      They operate exactly the same as the main class, using the concords u- and ba-,
      but they have an unusual plural (o-). They commence with u-, however, and
      most refer to people (but there are a few that do not).
      A few you need to know are as follows:

| | | | |
|---|---|---|---|
| nurse | unesi | ugesi | electricity |
| father | ubaba | doctor | udokotela |
| who? | ubani? | grandmother | ugogo |
| teacher | uthisha, uthishela | usikilidi | cigarette |
| mother | umama | | |

*Examples:*

   o    The doctor works in the hospital
        Udokotela usebenza esibhedlela
   o    Doctors work in the hospital
        Odokotela basebenza esibhedlela
        Father works but granny stays at home
        Ubaba uyasebenza kodwa ugogo uhlala ekhaya
        Electricity helps a lot
        Ugesi usiza kakhulu

76

## 50. Possessives (personal)

We deal here with the personal possessives: my, your, his, her, our, your (pl) and their and not with the possessives indicated by an apostrophe (e.g. the child of the woman = the woman's child).
Study the following sentences:

My child studies well    Umtwana *wami* ufunda kahle
Your child studies well    Umntwana *wakho* ufunda kahle
His/her child studies well    Umntwana *wakhe* ufunda kahle
Our child studies well    Umntwana *wethu* ufunda kahle
Your (pl) child studies well    Umntwana *wenu* ufunda kahle
Their child studies well    Umntwana *wabo* ufunda kahle

My dogs bite    Izinja *zami* ziyaluma
Your dogs bite    Izinja *zakho* ziyaluma
His/her dogs bite    Izinja *zakhe* ziyaluma
Our dogs bite    Izinja *zethu* ziyaluma
Your (pl) dogs bite    Izinja *zenu* ziyaluma
Their dogs bite    Izinja *zabo* ziyaluma

The following points emerge:
1. Unlike the English, where the possessive is a constant word which precedes the noun, in Zulu it follows the noun.
2. There are special groups of letters denoting my, your, etc. and these word endings are joined to the concord to give the harmonious sound which characterises the language. In the examples quoted, the concord of child (umntwana) is u- and this sound is carried into the wami, wakho etc. The concord of dogs (izinja) is zi- and the 'z' sound similarly features in zami, zakho, etc.
3. The possessives undergo modifications, as set out in the next paragraph, but the normal concord governing the action does not. In the first example above, the action is: child he study = umntwana ufunda. The wami, wakho, etc. only *describes* the child, and the main action 'ufunda' remains constant.
4. The word endings are:
   my -ami    your -akho       his/her -akhe
   our -ethu    your (pl) -enu    their -abo
   and when joined to the concord, the concord undergoes a slight change, as follows:
   (a) Single-letter concord: i becomes y and u becomes w
       This is really the result of a new *sound* which arises when an 'a' follows them in rapid speech, i.e.
       i + a = eeee ah = ya
       u + a = uuuu ah = wa
   (b) Two-letter concords: Drop the second letter:
       zi + a = za
       ba + a = ba
   (c) Linked to their concords, the words are thus as tabulated:

|  | My | Your | His/her | Our | Your pl | Their |
|---|---|---|---|---|---|---|
|  | -ami | -akho | -akhe | -ethu | -enu | -abo |

*I'm In class*
Concord:

|  |  | My | Your | His/her | Our | Your pl | Their |
|---|---|---|---|---|---|---|---|
| *Singular* i- | Possessive | yami | yakho | yakhe | yethu | yenu | yabo |
| *Plural* zi- | Possessive | zami | zakho | zakhe | zethu | zenu | zabo |

*You People class*
Concord:

|  |  | My | Your | His/her | Our | Your pl | Their |
|---|---|---|---|---|---|---|---|
| *Singular* u- | Possessive | wami | wakho | wakhe | wethu | wenu | wabo |
| *Plural* ba- | Possessive | bami | bakho | bakhe | bethu | benu | babo |

5.  Some examples of above:

house:  indlu (concord i-)      plural izindlu (concord zi-)

my house    house it-my       indlu i-ami = indlu yami
your house   it-your    indlu i-akho = indlu yakho
our house    it-our    indlu i-ethu = indlu yethu
our houses    houses they-our    izindlu zi-ethu = izindlu zethu
your (pl.) houses    they-your    izindlu zi-enu = izindlu zenu
their houses    they-their    izindlu zi-abo = izindlu zabo

boy: umfana (concord u-)      plural abafana (concord ba-)

my boy    boy he-my    umfana u-ami = umfana wami
her boy    boy he-her    umfana u-akhe = umfana wakhe
our boy    boy he-our    umfana u-ethu = umfana wethu
their boy    boy he-their    umfana u-abo = umfana wabo
your boys    boys they-your    abafana ba-akho = abafana bakho
their boys    boys they-their    abafana ba-abo = abafana babo

*Examples* in sentences:
o    Your dog is drinking water = dog it-your it-drink water
     Inja yakho iphuza amanzi
     Her child is crying = child it-her it-cry
     Umntwana wakhe uyakhala
     My boys are good = boys they-my they-good
     Abafana bami balungile
     Your cattle are eating grass = cattle they-your they-eat grass
     Izinkomo zakho zidla utshani
     I want to see your car = car it-your
     Ngifuna ukubona imoto yakho
o    They want to buy his fowls = fowls they-his
     Bafuna ukuthenga izinkukhu zakhe

6.  In any sentence there may be nouns of different classes and as these have
different concords, the possessive 'links' will of course be different. Remember
that the possessive describes the noun immediately in front of it, e.g. my dog is
biting your children = dog it-my it-bite children they-your = inja yami iluma
and then follows the object: children they-your = abantwana bakho. The full
sentence is thus:

78

o    Inja yami iluma abantwana bakho

Another example is:

His people like my goats = Abantu bakhe bathanda izimbuzi zami.

7.  The fact that the possessive is placed immediately after the noun and that the concord, in most cases, takes its sound from the noun must not lead the student to believe that the possessive concord is the one to apply in all subsequent linkages in the sentence. Remember that the amendment of the concord applies only to the *possessive* (which merely describes the noun) and that the *pure* concord governs the action itself, e.g.

My dog is drinking water = dog it-my it-drink water

Inja yami *i*phuza amanzi (not yaphuza)

## 51. Question: Whose?

This question arises naturally from the possessives, and the word to use is KABANI? (lit. of whom?). The noun comes first and the concord is not used unless it is a two-letter concord.

*Examples*:

Whose money?    Imali kabani?

Reply: Mine    Imali yami

Whose child?    Umntwana kabani?

Reply: Hers    Umntwana wakhe

Whose children?    Abantwana bakabani?

Reply: Hers    Abantwana bakhe

Whose affair?    Indaba kabani?

Reply: Theirs    Indaba yabo

Whose dogs?    Izinja zikabani?

Reply: Yours    Izinja zakho

Note:  See item 7 App II for more about the use of KA-.

## 52. Negatives of two noun classes

1.  Refer to paragraph 40 in which the 'negative table' is set out. We can now expand this table to include the 'I'm In' class.

The 'You People' class is already there because 'he, she and they' are in fact the concords of this class.

As in all negatives, A- is placed in front of the concord to indicate 'not', so that in the 'I'm In' class we have:

*Singular*:   a- + i- = ayi-

(the 'y' is a cushion that forms itself between the vowels a and i)

*Plural*:   a- + zi- = azi-

2.  A tabulated form of all the concords dealt with thus far, in both Positive and Negative, may be of assistance and is set out overleaf:

|         |                      | Positive |                   | Negative |
|---------|----------------------|----------|-------------------|----------|
| *Singular* | I                 | ngi-     | I do not          | angi-    |
|         | You                  | u-       | You do not        | awu-     |
|         | He/she (You People)  | u-       | He/she does not   | aka-     |
|         | It (I'm In)          | i-       | It does not       | ayi-     |
|         |                      |          |                   |          |
| *Plural* | We                  | si-      | We do not         | asi-     |
|         | You (pl.)            | ni-      | You (pl.) do not  | ani-     |
|         | They (You People)    | ba-      | They do not       | aba-     |
|         | They (I'm In)        | zi-      | They do not       | azi-     |

To complete the Negative, the usual change to the Verb takes place i.e.
Present Tense:    verb ends in -i
Future Tense:    -zo- becomes -zu-
Past Tense:    verb ends in -anga

*Examples*

(I'm In class only: for You People class, see paragraph 41).

The dog is drinking water    Inja iphuza amanzi
The dog is not drinking water    Inja ayiphuzi amanzi

The babies are crying    Izingane ziyakhala
The babies are not crying    Izingane azikhali

The cattle will return tomorrow    Izinkomo zizobuya kusasa
The cattle will not return tomorrow    Izinkomo azizubuya kusasa
The ox will not return tomorrow    Inkabi ayizubuya kusasa

o    The dog has gone    Inja ihambile
o    The dog has not gone    Inja ayihambanga
The dog went    Inja yahamba
The dog did not go    Inja ayihambanga

3.    For Negatives of Places, Conditions and Infinitive, the rules set out in
paragraphs 40, 42 and 43 apply in a similar fashion, using ayi- and azi- as being
applicable to the I'm In class, e.g.
*Place:*
The dog is not here    Inja ayikho lapha
The dogs are not here    Izinja azikho lapha
The dog is not in the garden    Inja ayikho engadini
*Conditions:*
The fowls are not hungry    Izinkukhu azilambile
The dog is not tired    Inja ayikhathele
*Infinitive:*
The infant does not want to drink
Ingane ayifuni ukuphuza
o    The dogs do not want to bite
Izinja azifuni ukuluma

# Exercise No. 13

(a) *Humusha ngesiZulu:*
1. The dog is drinking water.   2. The induna is calling the people.   3. Where are the cattle?   4. Why are the babies crying? They are hungry.   5. The boys want to hit the dog. Whose dog? My dog.   6. My car runs well.   7. The children are playing outside. Whose children? Her children.   8. Give the baby milk if it cries a lot.   9. Don't play with snakes because they bite people.   10. Your children are playing in my garden (= in garden it-my).

(b) *Humusha ngesiNgisi:*
1. Inja iphi manje? Angazi, ibalekile.   2. Indoda ifuna ukusebenza lapha.   3. Izinkomo zidla utshani entabeni.   4. Izinja zilume abantwana izolo.   5. Izinduna zizofika nabantu enkosini.   6. Intombazana ifuna ukusebenza efektri.   7. Ingane ikhalelani? Iyakhala ngoba ifuna ubisi.   8. Ziphi izimbuzi zami? Ziye emfuleni.   9. Abantu badla inyama kodwa izinkomo azidli inyama, zidla utshani.   10. Uphi umntwana wakho? Uye esikoleni.

(c) *Humusha ngesiZulu:*
1. The man does not work in an office, he works in a garage.   2. My dogs do not bite.   3. His cattle are here, they have not gone to the river.   4. Their fowls are no good, they make a noise.   5. The baby does not want to drink milk, it is not hungry.   6. My dogs do not like to bite, they just want to play.   7. Are the goats hungry? No, but they want water.   8. The chief does not want to talk to the people today.   9. The man does not work well, perhaps he is tired.   10. No, he is not tired, he is drunk.

(d) *Humusha ngesiNgisi:*
1. Imoto yami ayikho egalaji, iphi?   2. Izimpahla zakho zisetafuleni, azikho ekhabetheni.   3. Inyoni ayithandi inyama, ifuna isinkwa.   4. Siyajabula ngoba inyoka ayikho engadini, ihambile.   5. Izingane azilungile ngoba azifuni ukulala ebusuku.   6. Intombazana ayithandi ikhofi, iphuza itiye kuphela.   7. Abantu abadli utshani kodwa izinkomo zidla utshani.   8. Izimbuzi azidli inyama kodwa abantu bathanda inyama kakhulu.   9. Azikho izimbuzi engadini, zikhona izinja kuphela.   10. Izinja zakho azilungile ngoba ziyaluma.

# CHAPTER FOURTEEN

Counting
Money Terms, Buying and Selling

## 53. *Counting*

(i) Counting was traditionally done on the fingers, starting with the small finger of
the left hand, palm outward. The thumb of the right hand would thus be '6' and
this word (isithupha) means both thumb and six. The next finger (right index)
denotes '7' but also happens to be the 'pointing' finger and the word
'khombisa', on which 7 is based, does in fact mean to show or point out. The
numerals from 1 to 5 are adjectives which require the concord as link. They
are: 1 -nye  2 -bili  3 -thathu  4 -ne  5 -hlanu. From 6 onwards they are
nouns.
Counting in Zulu is not easy as the concords have variations which can be
confusing, and in this course we will use English numerals only (these are well
known to the average Zulu).

(ii) To express a number, use the English number (wani, thu, etc.) as follows:
noun + concord + ngu or wu + English equivalent.

*Examples:*

- o  the people are 8 = people they (be) 8
  abantu bangu 8 (or bawu 8)

  the sheep are 3 = sheep they (be) 3
  izimvu zingu 3 (or ziwu 3)

  the children are 57 = children they (be) 57
  abantwana bangu 57 (or bawu 57)

  the boy is only 1 = boy he (be) 1 only
  umfana ungu 1 kuphela

---

**Key to Symbols in text** to be used in conjunction with tapes:
- o    The word or sentence
- ▷    The complete line
- ►    The complete section

## 54. Money terms, buying and selling

(i)  The terms in use are:
    cent   isenti (concord li-) plural amasenti (concord a-)
    rand   irandi (concord li-) plural amarandi (concord a-)
Using English equivalents, plus ngu- or wu- as shown above, we thus have:
5 cents = amasenti a- + ngu + 5 = amasenti angu 5 (or awu 5)
12 rands = amarandi a- + wu- + 12 = amarandi awu 12 (or angu 12)

(ii) Rands and Cents. Using the word 'na' (and) to join cents to the word for rands
    (see paragraph 30) we get, e.g.
    ○  R3,50 = amarandi angu 3 namasenti angu 50
        R1,45 = irandi liwu 1 namasenti awu 45
        but in practice you will often hear the English version i.e. three rand fifty,
        one rand forty-five, and it is suggested this method be used to facilitate
        conversation.


*Price paid*

To buy or sell an item 'for' a certain sum is 'nga-' which means 'by means of'
(see paragraph 33). Fortunately the coalescence which 'nga-' employs does not
change it because amasenti and amarandi both start with a-.

*Examples*:
    Buy bread for 60 cents
    thenga isinkwa nga + amasenti angu/awu 60
    buy   bread   for    cents    they be   60
=   Thenga isinkwa ngamasenti angu/awu 60

    Buy a car for R2 500
    thenga imoto nga + amarandi awu/angu 2 500
    buy   car   for    rands    they be   2 500
=   Thenga imoto ngamarandi awu/angu 2 500

    Sell fowls for R4,25
    thengisa izinkukhu nga + amarandi angu/awu 4,25
    sell   fowls   for   rands   they be   4,25
=   Thengisa izinkukhu ngamarandi angu 4,25

*How much? What price?*

(i)  How much? is expressed by the word 'malini' which is literally what
    money?
(ii) The simplest way to establish the price is to say 'malini' followed by the
    item in question, e.g.
    malini ubhanana?   how much the bananas?
    malini ubhasikidi?   how much the basket?
    or by using lokhu (this thing), e.g.
    malini lokhu? (pointing to the item in question)
(iii) The word 'biza' (call) also means: cost, and the concord of the item must
    be used, e.g.
    ○  izinkukhu zibiza malini? = fowls they-cost how much?
        ubhanana ubiza malini? = the bananas it-cost how much?

The reply would be, e.g.
>
> zibiza amarandi awu 4 = they cost R4
>
> ubiza amasenti awu 80 idazini = they cost 80c dozen.

If the concord is not known, you could use lokhu (this thing) with the indefinite concord 'ku', e.g.

kubiza malini lokhu? = it costs how much this thing?

and the reply would similarly be:

kubiza amarandi/amasenti awu . . .

(iv)  Useful words in this connection are:

>
> kudulile (it is dear) and kushibhile (it is cheap)

(v)  Note that the word 'malini' is not confined to prices. It also applies to wages, e.g.

>
> o  UJoe uhola malini?
>
> Joe earns how much?
>
> Ufuna malini ukusebenza lapha esitolo?
>
> How much do you want to work here in the shop?


## Exercise No. 14

(a)  *Humusha ngesiZulu:*

1. The cattle are 12.   2. The people are 23.   3. My children are 3, your children are 5.   4. I will bring the money tomorrow. How much will you bring? I will bring R15.   5. The child is asking for 75 cents.   6. I will sell my car for R2 000.   7. Yesterday I bought clothes in town, they are cheap in town but dear at home.   8. How much are your goats? They cost R45.   9. How much does Joe earn? He gets R90 per week.   10. How much do the bananas cost? they cost 90c a dozen. That is very dear. OK, I will sell for 75 cents.

(b)  *Humusha ngesiNgisi:*

1. Abantu ebhasini bangu 45.   2. Izinkomo zami ekhaya zingu 11.   3. Kusasa ngizohola, ngizothola amarandi awu 85.   4. Ngakhokha (khokha = pay) amarandi awu 3 000 ngemoto yami.   5. Ubaba uthengisa izimbuzi ngamarandi angu 65.   6. Ngithanda ukuthenga izingubo eThekwini ngoba zishibhile khona (at that place).   7. We mfana, udayisani? Ngidayisa amathungulu. Ufuna malini? Ngifuna amasenti awu 50.   8. Abafana bafuna ukudlala ibhola kodwa uJames akafikanga, bangu 10 kuphela.   9. UMary uhola malini esitolo? Uhola kahle, uthola amarandi angu 500 ngenyanga.   10. Uma ngidayisile izinkukhu zami ngizothenga imbuzi yakho ngamarandi awu 40.

84

# CHAPTER FIFTEEN

To have or possess (and negative)
Some adverbs
Some adjectives
Indefinite 'it'
All, Only, Just

## 55. *To have or possess (and negative)*

(i) In paragraph 31 we saw that the way to express 'with, and' is NA- followed by Fusion. To 'have' in Zulu is based on the foregoing, since it is regarded as 'to be with', e.g. I have a car is expressed as: I am with car = I with car = ngi-na- + imoto = ngi-nemoto = nginemoto and it is written and pronounced as one word. Other examples:

We have food = we are with food = we with food
si-na- + ukudla = si-nokudla = Sinokudla

○ The child has a dog = child he (is) with dog
umntwana u- na- + inja = umntwana u-nenja = Umntwana unenja

(ii) Words that in English are loosely used in connection with possession, such as 'got, any, some' etc. are not normally expressed in Zulu, e.g.

I have got some sweets
would simply be: I with sweets
Ngi-na + amaswidi = Nginamaswidi
Have you any money?
You with money?
U-na + imali na? = Unemali na?

(iii) -PHETHE. This word, which is derived from phatha (to hold, handle) also has the meaning of 'Have' but in the physical sense, to hold in the hand, have on your person, etc., e.g.

○ Umuntu uphethe induku
The person has a stick (in his hand)
Abantwana baphethe imali
The children have money (on them)

but the NA- form may be used in this connection as well.

---

Key to Symbols in text to be used in conjunction with tapes:
○   The word or sentence
▷   The complete line
▶   The complete section

85

*Negative of 'Have'*

An unusual feature of this Negative is that the initial vowel of the following noun is dropped. The usual Negative Forms (angi- awu- aka- etc.) are used, as follows:

(1) *NA-* Note that there is no Fusion because the initial vowel of the noun following Na- falls away. Stated another way, the Negative of 'Have' is:

angina- awuna- akana- asina- anina- abana- without any fusion.

*Examples:*

○ We have no money = not we with money = Asinamali

They do not have a car = not they with car = Abanamoto

A Key Word to help remember:

○ Anginandaba meaning: I don't care, I have no interest (lit. I am not with the matter)

Mary has a child    UMary unomntwana

Mary has no child    UMary akanamntwana

The children have a garden at home

Abantwana banengadi ekhaya

The children do not have a garden at home

Abantwana abanangadi ekhaya

(2) *-PHETHE* This is added, unchanged, to the Negative Forms e.g.

I have no money (on me)    Angiphethe mali

The child has no sweets (in his possession)

Umntwana akaphethe maswidi

## 56. *Some adverbs of manner*

Study and learn the following words:

kahle    well, nicely, in a good way    (from: -hle    good, nice)

kabi    badly    (from: -bi    bad)

kakhulu    greatly, much, very, a lot    (from: -khulu    big)

○ kancane    a little, gently, gradually    (from: -ncane    small)

○ kangaki?    how many times, how often?    (from: -ngaki    how many?)

kanye    one time, once    (from: -nye    one)

kanyekanye    all together, all at one time

kabili    twice, again    (from: -bili    two)

kaningi    often, many times    (from: -ningi    many)

○ kanje    like this, in this manner    (from: -nje    of this sort)

kanjani?    how, in what manner?

   (from: -njani?    of what sort, in what condition)

kamnandi    pleasantly, sweetly    (from: -mnandi    pleasant, nice)

kalula    easily, lightly    (from: -lula    light, easy)

(i) It will be observed that using KA- in front of an adjective turns the latter into a corresponding adverb of manner (the way in which the action is done). The words on the right are all adjectives (describing something) and the words on the left are adverbs, describing how the action takes place.

*Examples*:

Uzobuya kangaki lapha?
How often will you return here?

o   Abafana bacula kamnandi
The boys sing sweetly

Ngiphuza kancane hhayi kakhulu
I drink a little, not much

UJane usebenza kanjani efektri? Usebenza kahle kakhulu.
How does Jane work at the factory? She works very well.

(ii)  The word 'kakhulu' meaning: greatly, very, much, is widely used. It can for
example be used after —
An action
Uphuza kakhulu    He drinks a lot
Another adverb
Basebenza kahle kakhulu    They work very well
Itself, to show intensity
Ngidinga imali kakhulu kakhulu    I need money very, very much

and is often used by itself to express assent to a question, e.g.

Can you speak English?    Uyakwazi ukukhuluma isiNgisi na?
Indeed I can    Kakhulu

## 57. *Some adjectives*

In the foregoing paragraph some adjectives were set out, but some of these are
not easy to use correctly as the concords often need amendment. Those quoted
below will be sufficient at this stage. See also paragraph 39 in which a few
conditions/states are given.

-lungile    good, nice, correct
-ngaki?    how many?
-ngcolile  dirty
-mnandi    pleasant, nice
-njani?    what sort, what condition?
-ningi   many
-mhlophe    white
-mnyama    black
-bomvu    red
-lula    light, easy

The concord is the link between the noun and the word describing it (the
adjective) and it must be used in front of the adjective, forming one word with it.

*Examples*:

The dog is black (or white)
Inja i + mnyama/mhlophe = Inja imnyama/imhlophe

The clothes are dirty
Izingubo zi + ngcolile = Izingubo zingcolile

○ The boy is how (what sort)?
Umfana u + njani = Umfana unjani?
○ He is all right
u + lungile = Ulungile

○ The fowls are how many? They are many
Izinkukhu zi + ngaki? Zi + ningi
Izinkukhu zingaki? Ziningi

The people are pleasant
Abantu ba + mnandi = Abantu bamnandi

Note: See item 8 App II for brief reference to adjectives used before the noun.

## 58. *To express: it is, there is*

(i) The word KU- means 'it' when not referring to a specific thing, i.e. it is the Indefinite. It is used with adjectives, with verbs, and with 'khona' (to be present).

(ii) *With Adjectives*: A few are given below:
-lungile   in order, good
-bi   bad
-shisa   hot
-makhaza   cold
-lula   easy, light
-nzima   heavy, difficult
-hle   good, nice
-nje   like this
-njalo   like that
-njani?   like what, what condition?
-lukhuni   hard, difficult
-ngcono   better

*Examples:*
Kulungile, buya kusasa   It is in order, come back tomorrow
Kuhle kakhulu (lokhu)   It is very good (this thing)
Kumakhaza namuhla   It is cold today
Kunjalo   It is so, it is like that, that is so

(iii) *With Verbs (Actions)* This expresses: It is . . . to . . . (action) e.g. it is good to . . . (rest) . . . with the 'to' being expressed by 'uku-'.

*Examples:*
○ It is good to work, it is bad to steal   Kuhle ukusebenza, kubi ukuntshontsha
It is easy to ride a bicycle   Kulula ukugibela ibhayisikili
It is difficult to speak Zulu well   Kunzima ukukhuluma isiZulu kahle

(iv) *With Khona* This expresses: There is (presence, availability, etc.)

*Examples:*
Kukhona inja lapha na?   Is there a dog here?
Kukhona isinkwa, hhayi ikhekhe   There is bread (but) not cake

(v) *Negative of KU-*

For all except with 'khona', the negative is formed by using the Negative Indicator A- in front of Ku- to give AKU-.

    It is so   Kunjalo

    It is not so   Akunjalo

○   It is not easy to drive a car   Akulula ukushayela imoto

    It is in order   Kulungile

    It is not in order   Akulungile

but note that the negative of 'kuhle' and 'kubi' take a double 'ku' i.e. akukuhle (it is not good) and akukubi (it is not bad), e.g.

    It is not good to steal   Akukuhle ukuntshontsha

With 'khona', the negative is shortened to -kho to become akukho.

*Examples:*

Akukho lokho = there is not that thing = That is not so, That is not true, That is nonsense.


## 59. To express: all, only, just

(a) *All* The word is -ONKE and it is used with the concord. As it starts with a vowel, the vowel of the concord is dropped, and we thus have:

Concord ba- : ba- + -onke = bonke

Concord zi- : zi- + -onke = zonke

Concord i- : i- + -onke = yonke (a new sound comes into being)

Concord si- : si- + -onke = sonke

The more common usage is to place this word in front of the noun but it makes no difference if you use it after the noun (a practice which is recommended because of the 'sound' connection between noun and concord, until the various concords are well known).

*Examples:*

    All the people want to go

    Abantu bonke (or: bonke abantu) bafuna ukuhamba

○   I will buy all the fowls

    Ngizothenga izinkukhu zonke (or: zonke izinkukhu)

    He took all the money

    Uthathe imali yonke (or: yonke imali)

○   We all like sweets

    Sonke sithanda amaswidi

(b) *Only, merely, just*

(i) This is expressed by the word KUPHELA (meaning: that is all) which is not linked to any concord but is a word on its own and usually at the end of the statement.

*Examples:*

    I only want George   Ngifuna uGeorge kuphela

○   He is only buying bread   Uthenga isinkwa kuphela

    They are calling me only   Babiza mina kuphela

○   We are only playing   Siyadlala kuphela

(ii) Another word having the meaning of Merely, Just and used in the same way as Kupehla is NJE.

*Examples:*

    The child does not want to run, he merely likes to sit
    Umntwana akafuni ukugijima, uthanda ukuhlala nje

  o  We are merely/just playing
     Siyadlala nje

## Exercise No. 15

(a) *Humusha ngesiZulu:*
1. We have bread and meat. 2. Have you (got) any money? 3. The man has a stick. 4. Mary has children at home, they are three. 5. I came many times last month. 6. The children sing sweetly in church. 7. The dog is vicious. 8. We have (some) fowls at home, they are white. 9. The children are many at school, some are big, others are small. 10. Jane will wash the clothes because they are dirty.

(b) *Humusha ngesiNgisi:*
1. We Tom, uyaphi? Ngiya esitolo. 2. Uphethe imali na? Yebo, ngiphethe imali. 3. Uphethe malini? Nginamarandi awu 2. 4. Abantwana abanye bafunda kalula, abanye bafunda kanzima. 5. Uthisha uvama (in the habit of) ukushaya thina abantwana ngerula emzimbeni, ushaya kathathu nje. 6. Inja imnyama kodwa izimbuzi zibomvu. 7. Umama unengadi ekhaya, uthanda kakhulu ukusebenza engadini yakhe. 8. Ubaba wakho unemoto na? Yebo, unemoto. 9. Imoto yakhe injani? Imhlophe. 10. Abantu banomsebenzi, baya emsebenzini wabo ngebhasi.

(c) *Humusha ngesiZulu:*
1. It is very hot in Zululand. 2. Tom is ill. Is that so? Yes, that is so. 3. Are there dogs in the yard? 4. It is good to work, it is not good to loaf. 5. It is not easy to speak Zulu well but we are trying. 6. There is food in the house. 7. All the people have gone to work. 8. The man does not want food, he only wants money. 9. I travel by bus only, I do not go by train. 10. The fowls are cheap, they only cost R4.

(d) *Humusha ngesiNgisi:*
1. Kulula ukugibela ibhayisikili kodwa akulula ukshayela imoto. 2. Thoko, uphasile na? Yebo, ngiphasile. Kuhle kakhulu lokho. 3. Qaphela, kukhona inyoka engadini. 4. Uthisha ufuna bonke abantwana bafike kusasa. 5. UDavid akasebenzi, uyalova nje. 6. Zonke izinkomo ziye emfuleni, zifuna amanzi. 7. Umfana akalungile ngoba uthathe imali yonke. 8. We nduna, siqedile umsebenzi. Kulungile, hambani-ke. 9. Abafana abafuni ukufunda esikoleni, bathanda ukudlala kuphela. 10. Nginemali namuhla ngoba izolo ngiholile.

# CHAPTER SIXTEEN

Verbs commencing with a vowel: Enza, Azi
Some demonstratives
Here is, here are
Can, should, ought to, must

## 60. *Verbs commencing with a vowel: -ENZA and -AZI*

There are not many verbs that commence with a vowel. Some are:
-azi   know
-akha   build
-enza   make, do
-eba   steal
-oma   be thirsty
-osa   fry, roast
We will in this course deal with only -azi and -enza.

(i) As we saw in paragraph 3, when no word follows the action, 'ya' is used between the concord and verb. With the sort of verb now under discussion, when using 'ya', the vowel of 'ya' falls away entirely.

*Example:*
Does he know? = he does know?
u + ya + azi na? = uyazi na?
Yes, he knows
yebo, uyazi

(ii) In other cases (where there is a word following) the 'ya' is of course not used, but the meeting of two vowels (in the concord and verb) causes modifications, as follows:
The single-letter concords u- and i- form a new sound to become w- and y- respectively.
The two-letter concords drop their vowels entirely.
We thus have:

|   |   | With ya | Without ya |
|---|---|---------|------------|
| I | ngi- | ngiyenza | ngi + enza = ngenza |

---

**Key to Symbols in text** to be used in conjunction with tapes:
   o    The word or sentence
   ▷    The complete line
   ►    The complete section

| | | | |
|---|---|---|---|
| You | u- | uyenza | u + enza = wenza |
| He/she | u- | uyenza | u + enza = wenza |
| It | i- | iyenza | i + enza = yenza |

| | | | |
|---|---|---|---|
| I | ngi- | ngiyazi | ngi + azi = ngazi |
| You | u- | uyazi | u + azi = wazi |
| He/she | u- | uyazi | u + azi = wazi |
| It | i- | iyazi | i + azi = yazi |

(I'm In class)

*Plural*

| | | | |
|---|---|---|---|
| We | si- | siyenza | si + enza = senza |
| You | ni- | niyenza | ni + enza = nenza |
| They | ba- | bayenza | ba + enza = benza |
| They | zi- | ziyenza | zi + enza = zenza |

| | | | |
|---|---|---|---|
| We | si- | siyazi | si + azi = sazi |
| You | ni- | niyazi | ni + azi = nazi |
| They | ba- | bayazi | ba + azi = bazi |
| They | zi- | ziyazi | zi + azi = zazi |

(I'm In class)

*Examples:*

○ Jane is making tea   UJane wenza itiye
The dogs are making a noise   Izinja zenza umsindo (or: zibanga umsindo)
What are you doing?   Wenzani wena?
What do you know?   Wazini wena?

(iii) With the infinitive UKU-, this becomes UKW- because of the sound that naturally arises when u is followed by a or e.

*Examples:*

I want to know   Ngifuna ukwazi
They want to make tea   Bafuna ukwenza itiye

(iv) *Negative of Vowel-Verbs*
Using the Negative Forms (angi- awu- aka- ayi- etc.) but with the amendments to single- and double-letter concords discussed in (ii) above, and with the negative tense indicators such as -i/-anga we thus get:
-Enza: angenzi  awenzi  akenzi  ayenzi
        *Plural*: asenzi  anenzi  abenzi  azenzi

-Azi: angazi (a well-known word!)  awazi  akazi  ayazi
        *Plural*: asazi  anazi  abazi  azazi

*Examples:*

Madoda, uGumede uyagula na? Mnumzana, asazi
Men, is Gumede ill? Sir, we don't know
○ Abantwana abenzi lutho, bayahlala nje
The children are not doing anything, they are just sitting around.

92

## 61. This, that, these, those

(i) There are three adjectives indicating position — close to the speaker, a short distance away, and quite a distance away, but still in sight. In this course we will deal with the first two only.

(ii) Whereas in English these demonstrative words apply to *any* noun, in Zulu they have a connection with the concord in their formation. The words are:

|  | Close to Speaker (this, these) | Short Distance Away (that, those) |
|---|---|---|
| You People class (concord *singular* u- | lo | lowo |
| *plural* ba-) | laba | labo |
| I'm In class (concord *singular* i- | le | leyo |
| *plural* zi-) | lezi | lezo |
| Indefinite 'ku' | lokhu | lokho |

(iii) They are individual words and not joined in their use to any concord (but see next paragraph (iv) regarding their position).

*Examples:*
○ Umfana lo usebenza kahle   This boy works well
○ Inja leyo iluma abantwana laba   That dog is biting these children

(iv) They are commonly used in front of the noun they describe, and in this case the initial vowel of the following noun is left out, e.g. lo mfana, laba bantu, lezi zinja.

*Examples:*
○ Lo mfana usebenza kahle   This boy works well
○ Leyo nja iluma laba bantwana   That dog is biting these children
  Ngifuna ukuthenga lezo zinkukhu   I want to buy those fowls

## 62. To express: here is, here are

There are words for three positions (here, there and yonder) but one position (here, near the speaker) is sufficient for this course:

| He/she | Concord u- | here he/she is | nangu |
|---|---|---|---|
| They | Concord ba- | here they are | naba or nampa |
| It | Concord i- | here it is | nansi or nayi |
| They | Concord zi- | here they are | nazi |
| Indefinite 'ku' |  | here it is | nakhu |

*Examples:*
○ Here is the child   Nangu umntwana
○ Here are the children   Naba/nampa abantwana
  Here is your money   Nansi/nayi imali yakho
  Where are the dogs? Here they are outside   Ziphi izinja? Nazi phandle

### 63. *To express: can (ability to do)*

(i) This is expressed by -YAKWAZI followed by UKU- (this is based on the verb -azi (to know) and is literally 'do it know to' i.e. know how to). It is used with concords.

*Examples:*

       Joyce can sew (knows how to)    UJoyce uyakwazi ukuthunga
  o  Can you drive a car?   Uyakwazi ukushayela imoto na?
  o  Yes, I can (I know how to)   Yebo, ngiyakwazi
       George can speak English   UGeorge uyakwazi ukukhuluma isiNgisi

(ii) The Negative is the usual Negative Form (angi- awu- aka- etc.) followed by -KWAZI UKU-. The 'ya' is not used in any Negative construction.

*Examples:*

       I cannot drive a car   Angikwazi ukushayela imoto
                  Not I know how — to drive — car
  o  The child cannot read   Umntwana akakwazi ukufunda
                  Child not he know how — to read

(iii) See item 9 App II for another way to express 'can'.

### 64. *To express: should, ought to, must*

(i) This is expressed by -FANELE UKU- (lit: fit to, appropriate to) and is used with the concord.

*Examples:*

       I ought to go now   Ngifanele ukuhamba manje
       You (pl) should help the induna   Nifanele ukusiza induna
  o  The child must learn properly   Umntwana ufanele ukufunda kahle

(ii) The Negative is the usual Negative Form (angi- awu- aka- etc.) and the Uku-is of course retained.

*Examples:*

       He ought not to drink a lot   Akafanele ukuphuza kakhulu
       We should not talk like this   Asifanele ukukhuluma kanje
       The people must not work tomorrow
       Abantu abafanele ukusebenza kusasa

(iii) When used with the indefinite 'ku', the meaning is:
It is required, it is appropriate, it should be, it is in order
but when used in this way it is not followed by uku- but by a verb ending in -e.

*Example:*

       They should go now = it is required they go now
       Kufanele bahambe manje

and in the Negative, use akufanele with the action also ending in -e.

*Example:*

       We ought not to stay = it is not appropriate we stay
       Akufanele sihlale

It is suggested that Kufanele and Akufanele be used merely to confirm/dissent e.g. in reply to a question.

*Examples:*

▷ Should we work tomorrow?   Sifanele ukusebenza kusasa na?
   Yes (it is required)   Yebo, kufanele
   No (it is not required)   Cha, akufanele

## Exercise No. 16

(a) *Humusha ngesiZulu:*

1. Children, don't make a noise.   2. My child (mntanami), please make the tea now.   3. What does he know, he knows nothing.   4. This boy studies well at school, but that boy does not study, he merely plays the fool (ganga).   5. I want to buy those fowls, how much are they?   6. Where is my money? Here it is.   7. The boy came yesterday and here he is outside again, he says he wants to buy mangoes (umango).   8. Where are the people today? Here they are, they are waiting outside.   9. This goat is white but that goat is black.   10. What are the dogs doing? Here they are, they are just playing, they are not biting.

(b) *Humusha ngesiNgisi:*

1. Nina madoda, nenzani manje? Mnumzana, siyasebenza, senza amatafula.   2. Lo muntu wazi konke kodwa lowo akazi lutho.   3. Inja yazi intombazana kodwa izoluma abanye abantu.   4. Laba bantwana bafunda kahle esikoleni.   5. Ufuna ukuthenga lezi zinkukhu noma lezo na?   6. Ngifuna lezi, zibiza malini?   7. Thatha nakhu uhambe, kusasa uzothola okunye (something else).   8. Nampa abantu phandle, bathi balambile.   9. Nazi izinkukhu, zidla uqadolo engadini.   10. Ngifuna ukhulume kahle, angithandi ukuzwa lokho.

(c) *Humusha ngesiZulu:*

1. Phyllis can read well.   2. This child can run fast.   3. Joseph cannot swim but the other boys can.   4. The teacher should help the children.   5. You should go now because you have finished the work.   6. Must we work tomorrow? Yes, you must.   7. A child ought to keep quiet when his parents are speaking.   8. Mary, you should not wash the clothes because they are not dirty.   9. Should the children make a noise like this? No, they should not.   10. I cannot speak Xhosa but I can speak Zulu.

(d) *Humusha ngesiNgisi:*

1. Uyakwazi ukushayela imoto na?   2. UJoseph akakwazi ukukhuluma isiNgisi.   3. Siyakwazi ukugibela ibhayisikili.   4. Uma behamba ngo 6 bafanele ukubuya ngo 12.   5. Umntwana akafanele ukuphuza unemenedi ufanele ukuphuza ubisi kuphela.   6. Ufanele ukufunda esikoleni hhayi ukuganga.   7. Ngiyakwazi ukusebenzisa umshini kodwa uPeter akakwazi.   8. Umuntu akafanele ukushayela imoto uma ephuzile.   9. Madoda, kufanele nihambe manje nibuye kusasa uma lingani.   10. Thisha, nangu umfana phandle, ufike kaningi uthi ufuna ukufunda lapha esikoleni.

95

# CHAPTER SEVENTEEN

Single-syllable verbs
Single-word questions
Time to . . ./Place to . . .
Stop and Wait

## 65. Single-syllable verbs

(i)    By now the student will have noticed that a few verbs contain one syllable only.
They are not many. Those you will find useful are:
    -dla    eat
    -fa    die
    -zwa    hear, feel
    -mba    dig
    -za    come
    -ma    stand
They take the normal infinitive uku-, e.g.
I want to hear    Ngifuna ukuzwa
Do you want to eat now?    Ufuna ukudla manje na?
(this word 'ukudla' is also the word for 'food')
but in the Command form (Imperative) they differ from other verbs (see
paragraph 12). They cannot stand alone but require yi- in front, e.g.

Yidla!    Eat!    Yimba umgodi! Dig a hole!
The plural form takes the usual -ni after the foregoing amendment, e.g.
Madoda, yimani lapho!    Men, stand over there!

(ii)    The Command form of -za (come) is yiza, as set out above, but another form:
Woza! Come! which is an exception, is more common.

(iii) -Za is frequently used instead of fika, see item 10 App II.

## 66. Single-word questions

Some questions are built into the verb, such as -phi (where?) -ni (what?) and -
elani (why?) (paragraph 9) and these can therefore not be used as single-word

Key to Symbols in text to be used in conjunction with tapes:
    o    The word or sentence
    ▷    The complete line
    ►    The complete section

96

questions. In a situation calling for single-word questions, such as an accident, any untoward occurrence, etc. the following questions will be of use:

*Where*? Kuphi? (lit. it is where) or Kuphi nendawo? (in what place)

*Why*? Kungani? (lit. Why is it?)

*What*? Yini? or Kuyini? (lit. it is what?)

Yini le? What is this? Yini lokhu? What is this?

Other query words are independent and can of course be used singly e.g.

*How*? Kanjani? *When*? Nini? *Who*? Ubani?

○ KWENZENJANI? or KWENZEKENI? is a most useful word, meaning: What happened, what's wrong, what's up, how come, how did it happen? etc.

## 67. *Time to . . . place to . . .*

These useful phrases are:

Time to . . . isikhathi soku . . . Place to . . . indawo yoku . . .

and are followed by the verb.

*Examples:*

time to rest isikhathi sokuphumula

place to rest indawo yokuphumula

time to eat isikhathi sokudla

place to sleep indawo yokulala

A practical use is with Kukhona (there is) e.g.

○ There is a place to wash Kukhona indawo yokugeza

The Negative is: Time (isikhathi) — asikho: Place (indawo) — ayikho

*Examples:*

○ There is no time to play Asikho isikhathi sokudlala

There is no place to sleep Ayikho indawo yokulala

## 68. *Stop, wait*

These two words are sometimes confused.

Stop doing a physical action, leave off, discontinue: Yeka

Stop, wait (physical motion), stand: Yima

*Examples:*

Stop that! Yeka lokho!

Stop talking (cease to talk) Yeka ukukhuluma

Stand still, you! Yima wena!

Stop there (stand, stay) Yima lapho!

The word 'yima' is also used on the phone:

Yima kancane = Hold on a while

# Recapitulation No. 3

Summary of items since recapitulation No. 2 (on page 58):

| | |
|---|---|
| **Negatives** (para. 40–43) | A- precedes Concord  angi- awu- aka- asi- ani- aba-<br>Present Tense: Verb ends in -i  abasebenzi<br>Future Tense: -zo- changes to -zu-  angizuhamba<br>Past Tense (both): verb ends in -anga  akabuyanga<br>Infinitive: Ordinary negative + uku<br>  angifuni ukuhamba<br>Whereabouts: Ordinary negative + -kho<br>  akakho/akekho  abakho/abekho |
| **If/When** (para. 44) | uma, but u and ba change to e and be<br>  uma ngifika  uma bekhala |
| **Think, Say, Be of Opinion** (para. 45) | cabanga + ukuthi  ngicabanga ukuthi bayagula<br>-thi plus actual words  bathi bazothola umsebenzi<br>-sho + njalo  ngisho/angisho njalo |
| **Wish, Hope, Request** (para. 46) | fisa, themba, cela, funa, tshela<br>uku- if speaker wishes  bafisa ukuhamba kusasa<br>ukuthi . . .-e  if another to act<br>tshela abantu ukuthi babuye kusasa |
| **Nouns** (para. 47–49) | Concords — 'sound' corresponds to prefix of noun<br>I'm In class conc. i- and zi-<br>inja iyaluma/izinja ziyaluma<br>You People class conc. u- and ba-<br>umfana uyafunda/abafana bayafunda<br>Sub-class conc. u and ba<br>udokotela uyafika/odokotela bayafika |
| **Possessives** (para. 50) | Concord plus -ami -akho -akhe -ethu -enu -abo<br>imali yami, umsebenzi wakho, izinja zakhe,<br>  abafana bethu |
| **Whose?** (para. 51) | Noun plus Kabani  imoto kabani?  izinja zikabani? |
| **Negatives of Nouns** (para. 52) | Action: angi- awu- aka- ayi-<br>  asi- ani- aba- azi-<br>inja ayilumi  izinja azizuluma<br>  inja ayilumanga<br>Place: Negative + -kho  inja ayikho  izinto azikho<br>Condition: Negative + condition  inja ayilambile<br>Infinitive: Negative + uku  izinja azithandi ukuluma |
| **Counting** (para. 53) | Noun plus concord plus wu/ngu<br>  abantu bangu 8/bawu 8 |

| | |
|---|---|
| Money Terms, Buying and Selling (para 54) | amasenti/amarandi    awu/angu: malini? biza malini? thenga nga/thengisa nga malini inkukhu? ibiza malini inkukhu?    ngifuna/ngidayisa ngamarandi awu 4 |
| Have, Possess (para. 55) | Subject + na + fusion: Phethe (have on the person) nginemoto    banemali    baphethe imali |
| Negative of Have (para. 55) | Usual negative + na (no fusion) or phethe asinamali    akaphethe nduku |
| Adverb of Manner (para. 56) | ka- plus adjective kahle    kabi    kakhulu    kancane    kaningi    kamnandi |
| Adjective (para 57) | Subject + concord + adjective inja imnyama    umfana ulungile    abantu baningi |
| It is/there is (para. 58) | ku- with adjective kulungile    kumakhaza    kumnandi    kukhona    kunjalo Negative    aku-    akulungile    akunjalo    akukho |
| All (para. 59) | Concord + -onke    sonke    bonke    zonke    yonke abantu bonke    zonke izinja    imali yonke |
| Only, Just (para. 59) | kuphela or nje    ngifuna isinkwa kuphela    uyadlala nje |
| Vowel Verbs (para. 60) | Concord (amended) with -azi    -enza angazi    uJane wenza itiye    abenzi lutho |
| This, that, those (para. 61) | lo/lowo    laba/labo    le/leyo    lezi/lezo    lokhu/lokho lo mfana    le nja    laba bantu    angifuni lokho |
| Here is/Here are (para. 62) | Nangu    naba/nampa    nansi/nayi    nazi    nakhu nansi imali    nampa abafana    nazi izinkomo |
| Can (Ability to) (para. 63) | Concord plus -yakwazi uku- uyakwazi ukushayela    bayakwazi ukukhuluma    isiZulu Negative: ordinary negative plus -kwazi uku- angikwazi ukushayela    abakwazi ukupheka |
| Should, Ought (para. 64) | Concord plus -fanele uku- bafanele ukusebenza    asifanele ukusala lapha |
| One-syllable verbs (para. 65) | Yima! Yizwani, madoda! |
| Single Questions (para. 66) | kuphi (where)    kungani (why)    yini (what)    kwenzenjani (what happened) |
| Miscellaneous (para. 67–68) | Isikhathi sokuhamba    indawo yokulala Yeka!    Yima! |

## Test:

Complete the following sentences:

1. (We don't want) ukusebenza ngoba si (are hungry).
2. UJoe (will not) buya namuhla.
3. Intombazana ikhona na? Cha, (she is not here), ayifikanga namuhla.
4. Ngifuna u-(bring) imali (when) ubuya kusasa.
5. Abantu ba-(say what?). Bathi (they are ill) bafuna (to go) esibhedlela.
6. Uma ufisa (to learn) isiZulu (you must) ukukhuluma nabantu.
7. (Where is) inyoka? (It is over there) engadini.
8. Izinja (my) azilumi kodwa izinja (your) ziyaluma.
9. Abantwana (his) bathanda ukudlala engadini (my).
10. Izinkukhu (your) zibiza malini? Ngifuna (R4).
11. U-(have) mali na? Yebo, nginamarandi (2).
12. (I have no time) sokukhuluma nawe ngoba ngi (in a hurry).
13. UDick usebenza (badly) kodwa uGumede usebenza (very well).
14. Izinja zakho zi-(black) noma (they are white) na?
15. (It is good) ukusebenza hhayi ukuhlala ekhaya nje.
16. Ufuna ukuthenga (all) izinkukhu na? Yebo, (they cost) malini?
17. Angifuni (all) abafana, ngifuna umfana (that one) kuphela.
18. UJoe (can ride) isithuthuthu kodwa (he cannot) ukushayela imoto.
19. Abantu (should not) ukushayela imoto (when they are drunk).
20. (Here is) imali yakho, (it is) amarandi awu 15 namasenti awu 75.

Answers to above:

1. asifuni, lambile  2. akazu  3. ayikho  4. lethe, uma  5. thini, bayagula, ukuya  6. ukufunda, ufanele  7. Iphi, ilapho  8. zami, zakho  9. bakhe, yami  10. zakho, amarandi awu 4  11. ne, awu 2  12. anginasikhathi, jahile  13. kabi, kahle kakhulu  14. mnyama, zimhlophe  15. kuhle  16. zonke, zibiza  17. bonke, lowo  18. uyakwazi ukugibela, akakwazi  19. abafanele, uma bedakiwe  20. Nansi (nayi), ingu (iwu)

# Appendix I

## SOME ZULU CUSTOMS

Some aspects of Zulu culture are set out below:

*Greeting*    Greetings and acknowledgments form an important part of Zulu culture. The usual greeting is Sawubona or Sakubona and is in the plural form (*we* see you) as it derives from the head of a household greeting a visitor on behalf of himself and members of the household. It is a standard greeting and is used on all occasions. A subordinate person, if he has not been greeted by his senior (the usual practice) is expected to take the first opportunity to extend a greeting. All greetings should be acknowledged.

*Eye Contact*    A child is taught to look down when addressing his elders, to speak quietly and to speak only when spoken to. An avoidance of a direct look (apart from an occasional quick glance to show that you have his attention) must therefore not be taken as a sign of shiftiness or guilt.

*Sitting Down*    On entering a room, after knocking and being told to enter or being invited inside, a Zulu will seat himself unobtrusively — this is expected of him and he does not wait to be told to sit. In their culture a subordinate should not physically be taller than his senior. If made to stand he feels uncomfortable and he should be allowed to sit for any interview or conversation of more than mere passing duration.

*Family Connections*    How often has time off been requested owing to the death of a 'father', only to have the same request repeated at later intervals. The explanation is the extended family system, whereby a man's father includes not only his biological father but also the latter's brothers.

*Belief in Witchcraft*    This is firmly engrained, although perhaps to a lesser degree today than before. It should never be ridiculed.

*Finger-Pointing*    Pointing a finger at a person used to be a challenge and should be avoided. It is also considered very rude to wag a finger when scolding.

*Gratitude*    is often expressed by gestures rather than words, e.g. a clapping of the hand together, or a slight curtsy, but thanks should always be said in one way or another.

# USEFUL TELEPHONE PHRASES

| | |
|---|---|
| To phone, to ring somebody: | Shaya ucingo, shaya uthelefoni |
| To answer the phone: | Phendula ucingo, phendula uthelefoni |
| Hullo: | Halowo |

○ Who is that speaking — Ubani lo okhulumayo or ngikhuluma nobani?

This is . . . speaking — U . . . lapha

I want to speak to . . . — Ngicela ukukhuluma no. . .

Is he there? — Ngabe ukhona? or Ngingamthola?

Please call him. — Ngicela ubize yena or ngicela ungibizelele yena.

I am sorry he is not here. — Ngiyaxolisa akekho.

Please tell him Mr . . . rang. — Ngicela umtshele ukuthi ushayelwe Mr . . .

Please ask him to phone me back. — Ngicela umtshele angifonele futhi.

The number is . . . — Inombolo ithi . . . inamba ithi . . .

○ What is your number? — Ithini inamba yakho?

When will he be back? — Uzobuya nini?

Please tell him I will phone again later. — Ngicela umtshele ukuthi ngizobuya ngimshayela esikhatini esizayo.

○ Hold on, I am calling him. — Yima kancane, ngiyambiza.

Can somebody else help you? — Angakusiza omunye?

I will call someone else, please hold on. — Ngicela ume, ngibiza omunye

I won't be long. — Angizulibala.

There is nobody by that name here. — Akekho muntu obizwa ngalelo gama lapha.

You have the wrong number. — Udukile, ushaye ucingo lapho kungekhona.

What number did you ring? — Ubushaye iphi inamba?

○ Who do you want to speak to? — Ufuna ukukhuluma nobani?

Where are you speaking from? — Umaphi la or (lapho) ukhuluma khona?

I will tell him you rang. — Ngizomtshela ukuthi ubumshayelile.

Goodbye — Sala kahle

Thank you — Ngiyabonga

Did anyone phone while I was out? — Kukhona oshaye ucingo ngisaphumile na?

Who was it, what is his number? — Bekungubani? Ithini inombolo yakhe?

# ADDITIONAL READING AND EXERCISES

Funda indaba (Read the story):

## 1. Joseph Gumede

UJoseph Gumede uhlala eMlazi usebenza efektri eThekwini. Uvuka ngo-5 ekuseni kodwa hhayi zonke izinsuku ngoba ngesinye isikhathi usebenza ebusuku. Uthanda kakhulu ukusebenza ebusuku, uthi uhola kahle futhi emini uthola isikhathi sokuthenga izinto esitolo. Ukuya emsebenzini uhamba ngebhasi noma ngesitimela, ngesinye isikhathi uhamba ngetekisi. Uhola ngesonto yena kodwa abanye bahola ngenyanga. Emsebenzini bathola itiye nesinkwa ngesikhathi beqala ukusebenza futhi baphuza itiye ngo-10. Badla ilantshi ngo pasi 12 bashayisa ngo-5. Ufika ekhaya ngo-7.

Phendula imibuzo (answer the questions):
(a) UJoseph uhlalaphi, futhi usebenzaphi?
(b) Uvuka nini?
(c) Uvuka ekuseni zonke izinsuku na?
(d) Uthandelani ukusebenza ebusuku?
(e) Uhamba ngani ukuya emsebenzini?
(f) Uhola ngesonto noma ngenyanga na?
(g) Badlani emsebenzini?
(h) Badla nini ilantshi?
(i) Ushayisa ngasikhathi sini?
(j) Ufika nini ekhaya?

## 2. Ingadi yethu (our garden)

We have a garden at home at Ndwedwe. Mother likes our garden a lot, she works there (khona) every day. She wakes early and prepares breakfast because we start (enter) school at 7.30. We all go to school on foot because it is nearby. After that (emva kwalokho) mother works in the garden. She plants vegetables (imifino) and flowers and fruit (izithelo). Sometimes she sells fruit and eggs.

At home we have fowls and goats but mother is very cross if they come into the garden because they do damage (umonakalo) there (khona), the fowls scratch (phanda) the ground and the goats eat the vegetables.

On Saturday I help mother in the garden. My sister Dudu also helps but she herself likes very much to work in the house, she likes to bake cakes, she also makes tea or coffee. Mother drinks a lot of tea but I myself like coffee. Dudu only drinks Coke.

## 3. Shopping trip

Kusasa sizovuka ngo-5 ngoba sifuna ukuya edolobheni, sifuna ukuthenga ezitolo (izitolo is plural of isitolo). Sizohamba ngebhasi ngoba sifuna ukufika ekuseni edolobheni. Abantu baningi ebhasini, bonke baya edolobheni ngoMgqibelo bafuna ukuthenga ezitolo ngoba izinto zishibhile khona. Abanye bazothenga ukudla, abanye bazothenga izingubo, abanye inyama, abanye utshwala nogologo. Mina angizuthenga ukudla, ngifuna izicathulo kuphela. Umfowethu uzothenga isigqoko. Ubaba akafuni ukuthenga lutho, uthi uzobuka nje ngoba akanamali. Umama ufuna inyama namazambane noshukela nerayisi. Udadewethu ufuna ukuthenga irekhodi. Izitolo zizovala ngo-1 bese sibuyela (return to) ekhaya, sizobuya ngesitimela ngoba kushibhile esitimeleni. Ekhaya sizophuza itiye bese siya ebholeni.

Phendula imibuzo:
(a) Sizoyaphi kusasa?
(b) Sizohambelani ngebhasi?
(c) Abantu bazothengani?
(d) Ngizothengani mina? Umfowethu uzothengani yena?
(e) Ubaba uzothengani?
(f) Izitolo zivala nini edolobheni?
(g) Uma sibuyela ekhaya sihamba ngani? Kungani?
(h) Sizoyaphi ntambama?

## 4. James, Velaphi and Themba

JAMES:   Good-morning Velaphi, how are you?
VELAPHI:   Good-morning James. I am well. How are you?
JAMES:   I too am well.
(Themba comes into view)
Here is Themba.
THEMBA:   Good-morning, friends. How are you?
J & V:   Good-morning Themba. We are well. How are you?
THEMBA:   I'm O.K. Where are you going?
JAMES:   We are going to buy at the shop then go to the Post Office because Velaphi wants to phone.
THEMBA:   I too want to phone, I want to tell my brother that I will come to him in Johannesburg on Moday. I will go by train. Do you know that I have a job in Johannesburg?
VELAPHI:   We are glad to hear that. We ourselves are going to Durban, I have got a job at a garage in Jacobs, I start on Tuesday. James also hopes to get work in Durban.
JAMES:   That is so. My brother Dick works at a factory in Mobeni, he says I should come soon, perhaps I will find work.
THEMBA:   That is very good. I hope everything goes well. Goodbye my friends.
J & V:   Goodbye Themba, safe arrival in Johannesburg.

# ANSWERS TO EXERCISES

*Exercise No. 1* (page 7)

(a) 1. Ngibona inja  2. Sithanda ubisi  3. UJohn usebenza eThekwini  4. Bapheka inyama  5. Ubaba uyageza  6. Ngiyadla  7. Ulala kakhulu  8. Babiza uGeorge  9. Sidlala emini  10. Uyakhala

(b) 1. I like bread a lot  2. Mary drinks milk  3. They stay at Mlazi  4. They are playing  5. Annie is bringing tea  6. You read/he reads well  7. The child is eating  8. Father wants work  9. I am washing  10. Lettie is cooking meat

(c) 1. Uhlala eMlazi na?  2. Cha, ngihlala kwaMashu  3. UGeorge uyasebenza na?  4. Yebo, uyasebenza  5. Baphuza itiye kakhulu na?  6. Cha, bathanda ubisi  7. Uyasebenza na?  8. Cha, ngifuna umsebenzi  9. uMary upheka inyama na?  10. Cha, udla isinkwa

(d) 1. Do you work?  2. Yes, I work in Durban  3. Do the children play nicely?  4. Yes, they play nicely  5. Does Dlamini eat meat?  6. Yes, he likes meat a lot  7. Is Mary bringing tea?  8. No, she is bringing coffee  9. Do you like Khumalo?  10. No, I like Dlamini

*Exercise No. 2* (page 11)

(a) 1. Siyasebenza kodwa uTom uyageza  2. UJoe uthanda itiye futhi uthanda ubisi  3. Ngigeza ekuseni kodwa uGeorge ugeza ebusuku  4. Babiza uJohn futhi bafuna uSipho  5. ULettie uyakhala ngoba ufuna amaswidi  6. Ufuna ukusebenza noma ufuna ukudlala na?  7. Sithanda ukudla inyama kodwa bathanda ukuphuza itiye  8. Ngifuna ukulala manje  9. UDudu uyakhala ngoba ufuna ukuphuza ubisi  10. Bathanda ukusebenza eThekwini

(b) 1. I am washing but Joseph is drinking tea  2. They want tea, they also want bread  3. Do you/does he like tea or milk?  4. I wash in the morning/early because I work during the day  5. Joyce wants to cook meat  6. Do you like meat?  7. Yes, I like meat, I also like bread  8. Joe likes to stay at home but I like to work  9. Is Mary bringing tea or milk?  10. We are trying to learn Zulu

(c) 1. u, kodwa, u: Dick is drinking tea but Joseph is playing outside  2. Sifuna uku: We want to buy potatoes at the shop  3. uthanda: The child likes sweets  4. noma u: Do you work or do you stay at home?  5. Abantwana bayakhala, bafuna ubisi: The children are crying because they want milk  6. Ufuna, lapha na: Do you want to stay here?  7. ba, uku: The boys like to play a lot  8. ukufunda, sifuna ukukhuluma: We like to learn Zulu because we want to speak well  9. bathanda, noma: Do they like tea or coffee?  10. futhi ngithenga: I am buying meat at the shop and I am also buying bread

*Exercise No. 3* (page 16)

(a) 1. UJoe ufunani?  2. Bafundani?  3. Umntwana udlani?  4. Uthanda ukuphuzani?  5. UJane ulethani manje?  6. Umntwana ucelani?  7. Uthanda ukufundani ebusuku?  8. UGeorge uthanda ukusebenza emini noma uthanda ukusebenza ebusuku na?  9. Ubonani lapho?  10. Balethani namuhla?

(b) 1. What is Mary cooking now?  2. What does George like to eat?  3. What are the people reading/learning?  4. What are the people buying at the shop?  5. What does Joseph want to read at home?  6. What does father like to drink at night? 7. What do you see over there outside? 8. What is Jane washing in the kitchen? 9. What do the people eat at home, and what do they drink? 10. What do you/does he want here?

(c) 1. Ulalaphi ebusuku? 2. Abantwana badlalaphi? 3. Uthanda ukuhlalaphi? 4. Bafuna ukusebenzaphi? 5. UJoe ukhona na? Yebo, ukhona 6. Kodwa uphi? Usengadini 7. Abantwana baphi? 8. Badlala phandle engadini 9. Abantu bakhona (lapha) namuhla na? Cha, abekho 10. Baphi? Basekhaya

(d) 1. Where do you/does he stay now? 2. Where do the people like to work? 3. Where is Mary cooking meat? She cooks in the kitchen 4. The people are at home 5. Where is George? He is outside 6. Are the people at work? 7. Yes, they are at work 8. Where are the children? They are outside 9. Is Joseph present today? No, he is not 10. Where is he? I don't know

(e) 1. Sisebenzelani? 2. Siyasebenza ngoba sifuna imali 3. Umntwana uhlekelani? Ngoba ubona ikati 4. Abantu bafunelani imali? 5. Ngoba bafuna ukuthenga isinkwa 6. Bafundelani isiZulu? 7. Ngoba bafuna ukukhuluma kahle 8. Uthandelani ukulala emini/uthanda ukulalelani emini? 9. Ngoba ngisebenza ebusuku 10. Bafuna ukubalekelani/bafunelani ukubaleka? Ngoba babona inja

(f) 1. Why are you bringing money? 2. Because I want to give Joe money 3. Why do you work at night? 4. Because I get money a lot (much) 5. Why do the children want to go now? 6. Because they want to play football 7. Why does Joe like to read at night? 8. Because he works during the day 9. Why is the child running away? 10. He is running away because he sees a snake

*Exercise No. 4* (page 22)

(a) 1. Biza umntwana manje 2. Ngicela ubize umntwana manje 3. Mary, ngicela ubize uJoseph 4. Joyce, shanela ehhovisi bese ulungisa 5. Ngifuna uthathe amasheke uye ebhange bese ubuya nemali 6. Musa ukuthola upetroli 7. Musa ukuthola u-oyile egalaji uthole upetroli kuphela 8. We George, siza umntwana lapho 9. Yeka — bo 10. Kulungile-ke, hamba manje ubuye kusasa

(b) 1. I want you to sweep the shop early 2. Don't speak a lot 3. Mary, please bring the tea now because we want to go to the bank 4. Dlamini, go now and come back this afternoon and bring the money 5. Keep quiet, I say 6. Children, learn well at home then return to school tomorrow 7. Don't give the child sweets, it wants milk 8. Open the office early then open the windows and go to the post office 9. George, I want you to come back this afternoon 10. Khumalo, don't bring the book, I want you to bring the pencil

*Exercise No. 5* (page 27)

(a) 1. Ngicela ungene uhlale 2. Ungubani igama lakho? 3. Uyakwazi ukukhuluma isiNgisi na? 4. Sawubona Dlamini, unjani namuhla? 5. Ngiyaphila (ngisaphila) mnumzana, unjani wena? 6. Nami ngiyaphila. Kunjani ekhaya? 7. Kuhamba kahle. Ngicela ukubona uJoyce 8. Ngiyadabuka, uJoyce akekho namuhla 9. Uvelaphi/uphumaphi? Ngiphuma eNdwedwe 10. Ngiyahamba, sala kahle — hamba kahle

(b) 1. Goodmorning Khumalo, how are you today? 2. Do you know (speak) English? 3. Would you like (drink) tea or coffee? 4. What is your name? 5. Goodbye Sipho — goodbye sir 6. See you tomorrow! 7. Dlamini, where do you come from? 8. I come from Empangeni, sir 9. Come inside, please sit down 10. Thank you

*Exercise No. 6* (page 32)
(a) 1. Abantwana bathanda ukuya esikoleni 2. UJohn uhamba manje 3. Ngicela uye ebhange uthole imali 4. Umntwana uhamba kahle 5. Abafana bafuna ukugijima, hhayi ukuhamba 6. Ngicela ubeke ibhuku lapha hhayi etafuleni 7. UJoseph ufunda kahle esikoleni kodwa wena uyaganga 8. UTom uphi? Usiza mina kakhulu 9. Utisha uthanda ukushaya thina 10. Ubaba ufuna ukunika uTom imali ngoba uthanda yena kakhulu

(b) 1. I like to travel during the day, not at night 2. The children are going to school 3. I am going, goodbye 4. The people are going to the shop because they want to buy 5. Go now, don't come back 6. I like tea, not coffee 7. Sipho smokes a lot but I myself smoke a little 8. Father is calling you 9. Stop it! Don't hit the child 10. Very well, go now and come back tomorrow

*Exercise No. 7* (page 39)
(a) 1. Ngizobiza wena khona manje 2. UJoe uzobuya ngoMsombuluko 3. Uzoletha imali kusasa na? 4. Bazohamba ngo 7 babuye ngo 2 ntambama 5. Ngesonto elizayo ubaba uzothenga imoto 6. Abantwana bazosiza engadini ngoMgqibelo 7. Abantu bazothenga isinkwa noma inyama na? 8. Ubaba uzogeza imoto kusasa 9. Sizothola imali ntambama 10. Umfowethu uzoya ekhaya ekupheleni kwenyanga

(b) 1. Will you go? No, I will stay 2. Father will return soon 3. The people will buy tomorrow 4. I will come on Thursday not on Friday 5. The child will buy sweets 6. We will get money at the end of the month 7. Will Dlamini return on Monday? 8. No, he will come on Tuesday 9. The boys will play football in the afternoon 10. I will buy a car next month

(c) 1. UTom ufikile na? 2. Yebo, ufikile, ufike ngo 8 3. Ngisebenze izolo hhayi kuthangi 4. Sibone yena ekuseni esitolo 5. Badlile namuhla na? 6. Bahambe ekuseni na? 7. Abantwana baye esikoleni namuhla 8. Abantu baqale ngo 7 baqeda ngo 5 9. UGeorge ukhulume kakhulu izolo ebusuku 10. Umntwana uyakhala ngoba uMary uhambile

(d) 1. I came yesterday 2. Where is Joe? He has gone 3. He went at 11 o'clock 4. Did you work yesterday? Yes, I worked 5. The children are not at home, they have gone to school 6. Mary came early 7. Have you finished? 8. Yes, we have finished, we want to go 9. Have the people drunk? 10. Yes, they drank tea at 10 o'clock

(e) 1. Ngafunda eNdwedwe 2. Ngonyaka odlule ngahlala ekhaya 3. Abantu batshala amazambane ngonyaka odlule 4. Watshala ngenyanga edlule na? 5. Cha, ngatshala ummbila ngesonto eledlule 6. Ngabona uKhoza ekupheleni kwenyanga 7. Sathenga imoto ngesonto eledlule 8. Wafunda isiNgisi esikoleni na? 9. Yebo, ngafunda isiNgisi 10. UTom wakhulela eMbumbulu

(f) 1. I went last year   2. I returned last month   3. I started to work last week   4. Peter, where did you go to school (study)? I studied at Empangeni   5. Men, what did you buy last month?   6. We got money at the end of the month   7. Last year the child studied well but this year he is fooling   8. Where did Tom grow up?   9. He grew up in town   10. Last week I stayed at home

(g) 1. Ngiyahamba, ngizohamba, ngihambile, ngahamba   2. Basebenza namuhla, bazosebenza kusasa, basebenze izolo, basebenza ngenyanga edlule   3. UJoe uzofika kusasa, hhayi ngoLwesine   4. Ngitshele uGumede namuhla ekuseni futhi ngizotshela uKhumalo ebusuku namuhla   5. Ngesonto eledlule saletha inyama, ngalelisonto siletha isinkwa, ngesonto elizayo sizoletha itiye   6. Ngabona uDlamini ekhaya ngenyanga edlule   7. Uzohamba manje na?   8. Cha, ngizohamba ntambama ngo 3   9. Madoda, niqedile na?   10. Cha, sizoqeda ngo 5

(h) 1. Next month I will look for work in Durban   2. Last year I bought a car   3. The boys are happy because this afternoon they will play football   4. Has Dick returned? No, he will return tonight   5. Mary shopped in town this morning, she will return home this afternoon   6. We will finish the work at 5 o'clock   7. Jacob will visit Doris in hospital this afternoon   8. The doctor came at the end of the month, he will come again tomorrow   9. Last month father rested at home, next month he will return to work   10. Dick, are you staying? (yini = or what?) No, I will go soon

(i) 1. We bafana, nidlalephi izolo? Nadlalaphi ngesonto eledlule?   2. Abantwana bathengeni esitolo?   3. Umntwana ukhaleleni ebusuku?   4. Usebenzephi izolo?   5. Bafundani namuhla futhi bafundeni izolo?   6. Udlile na? Uma kunjalo, udleni?   7. Wahlalelani ekhaya ngenyanga edlule?   8. Wafundaphi ukukhuluma isiNgisi? Ngafunda esikoleni   9. Abantu bayephi? Baye esitolo, bathenga isinkwa   10. Uzolethani kusasa?

(j) 1. Say, Khoza, where did you go this morning? I went to the shop   2. What did you buy? I bought tobacco   3. Why did you buy tobacco, not bread? Because I smoke   4. Last year where were you at school? (did you study)   5. Where did you eat today? I ate at home, I also drank tea at work   6. What will the children buy at the tearoom? They will buy sweets   7. Where will you go tomorrow? I will go to town   8. Where did you stay last month? I stayed at home   9. Where did Tom grow up? He grew up in Zululand   10. Why has Joyce gone to hospital? Because she is sick

*Exercise No. 8*   (page 43)

(a) 1. Joseph, uqala nini umsebenzi?   2. Abantwana baya nini esikoleni?   3. UDick uzoya nini eThekwini?   4. UMary ufike nini? Ufike ekuseni ngo 6   5. Bafuna ukuya esitolo. Bafuna ukuhamba nini? Bazobuya nini?   6. UTom uhambile na? Uhambe nini?   7. Namuhla kusithibele, ngithi lizona   8. Uthi izulu lihle na? Mina ngithi izulu libi   9. KwaZulu kuyaduma kakhulu   10. Uma lina kakhulu abantwana bahlala ekhaya

(b) 1. When do the people get paid? They draw their pay on Friday afternoon   2. When do the children come home from school? They return at 3 p.m.   3. When do you wake up in the morning?   4. When do you start (to) work, when do you finish?   5. Where is Joe? He has gone. Where did he go? He went to the shop. What does he want at the shop? He wants tobacco. When will he return? He will come back soon   6. The weather is nice today because it is fine and warm   7. It is overcast today, also it is windy   8. Do you think it will rain?   9. I don't know, perhaps (the) rain will come this afternoon   10. When it rains we stop working outside, we come inside

*Exercise No. 9*   (page 49)

(a)   UJoe uthenga isinkwa, itiye (or: netiye) nobisi esitolo   2. Abantwana bafunda isiNgisi nesiZulu esikoleni   3. Ngifuna uAlbert, uGeorge (or noGeorge) noPeter   4. UMary uthanda itiye noshukela nobisi namanzi ashisayo   5. Umntwana udlala phakathi naphandle ngoMgqibelo   6. Ngicela uhambe nomntwana, ufuna ukuthenga amaswidi   7. Musa ukudlala nenyoka   8. UPeter ukhuluma noMary phandle   9. Ufuna ukuya nami edolobheni ntambama na?   10. Abantu baphandle, udokotela uzokhuluma nabo khona manje   11. UDick usebenza efektri nami futhi   12. Udokotela ufuna ukujova mina nawe futhi

(b)   1. Children like cakes and sweets but I myself like meat and bread   2. What is Joe buying at the tearoom? He is buying tobacco. What else? He is buying matches   3. Call Gumede and Cele and Vilakazi   4. Mother is going to the shop and will return with bread and sugar and potatoes   5. Say, George, who are you talking to outside?   6. Mother goes to town on Tuesday and Saturday   7. Father is preparing a place in the garden because he will plant vegetables here and here and over there   8. Mary, who will you go with to town? I will go with Ida   9. Joe is learning English, I too am learning English and Zulu   10. Where is Koza? I want to talk to him

(c)   1. UDick uya emsebenzini ngesitimela nami futhi, kodwa uTom uhamba ngebhasi   2. Siya edolobheni ngebhasi ngo Mgqibelo   3. Ngesonto abantu baya esontweni ngemoto nangezinyawo   4. Mary, ufika ngani eThekwini? Ngihamba ngebhasi   5. Abantwana baya ngani esikoleni? Bahamba phansi (or ngezinyawo)   6. Uthisha uthanda ukushaya thina, ushaya ngesandla   7. UDingane wabulala uShaka ngomkhonto   8. Uhola ngenyanga na? Cha, ngihola ngesonto   9. Umntwana usebenza engadini edolobheni ngoMgqibelo, uhola ngelanga   10. Ngenyanga edlule uJoe wahola kakhulu ngoba wasebenza ebusuku nantambama

(d)   1. My brother travels by car but I myself travel by motorbike   2. How did you come here? I came by bicycle   3. When did you arrive? I came at 3 o'clock   4. The person is cutting the tree with an axe   5. The children are hitting the dog with stones   6. I will tie up the parcel with string   7. Joe is hitting the metal with a hammer   8. How do you get paid? I am paid by the month but my brother is paid by the week   9. When does he get his pay? He is paid at 4 p.m. on Friday   10. The people go to town by train. How will they return? They will come back by bus.

(e)   Story (Ngempelasonto)   On the Weekend: Many people rest at home on the weekend. They stop work on Friday afternoon and return to work early on Monday. On Saturday we usually go to town, I go with mother and father and brother. We go by bus because we want to arrive early in town. Many people also like to go to town on Saturday, they want to buy in the shops. Some buy food, others buy clothes, others buy shoes, but I myself buy sweets and cakes. We return home at 1, we travel by train or taxi. In the afternoon we rest at home. Some like to play football, others work in the garden or in the house. We children help (our) parents. On Sunday we usually go to church, we go at 9 and return home at 11. To go to church we go on foot because it is nearby. On Sunday afternoon some play football, others read the paper, others go visiting. It is very nice to rest on the weekend.

(f) Second story: Sipho and Mother. Sipho: Mother, I ask to go to the soccer Mother: Who will you go with? Sipho: I will go with James and Mandla Mother: How will you go? Sipho: We will go on foot because it is near. Mother, I also ask for some money Mother: What do you want money for? Sipho: We pay to enter at the soccer, also I will buy lemonade or Coke because the day is very hot Mother: You are always wanting money! Allright. When will you return? Sipho: We will come back at 6. Thank you. Goodbye mother Mother: Goodbye, Sipho

*Exercise No. 10* (page 57)

(a) 1. Ngicela ukhiphe ibhuku ekhabetheni 2. Ufaka imali esikhwameni 3. Sithanda ukuthenga izingubo endaleni 4. Umntwana uwile, ulimele engalweni 5. Abantu abanye bathanda ukusebenza edolobheni, abanye bathanda ukuhlala emaphandleni 6. Uya emsebenzini na? Cha, ngiya ebholeni 7. UDick uchithe imali kakhulu emjahweni 8. Kukhona ukudla esitsheni 9. Uthanda ukusebenza endlini na? Cha, ngithanda ukusebenza phandle engadini 10. Abantu bahlala elangeni namuhla ngoba kumakhaza

(b) 1. Khoza works in a garage in town 2. Mary works for (at) Checkers on the Berea in Durban 3. Where does she stay? She stays at the hostel but goes home to Umzumbe on the weekend 4. Where is Dick today? He has gone to court, he will return this afternoon 5. Some people like to work in an office, others like to work in a factory 6. Dube will get a permit from the chief because he wants to plant sugarcane 7. The children are happy because they are going to the sea today 8. There is a fly in the milk in the bucket 9. Father stays at the homestead at Umbumbulu 10. Mr Jones returned from London last month

(c) 1. Ngiya kuthisha ngoba ufake isihlabathi enkomishini 2. Baphuza kakhulu kwaJoseph ngempelasonto 3. Uya enkosini na? Cha, uya enduneni kuqala 4. Umfowethu wasebenza eCape Town ngonyaka odlule kodwa manje ufuna umsebenzi eMgungundlovu 5. UMary usebenza kanjani efektri? Usebenza kahle, bathanda yena kakhulu 6. Umntwana ukhuluma kanjani? Ukhuluma kahle ngesiZulu kodwa ukhuluma kabi ngesiNgisi 7. Ubaba uthukuthele ngoba uTom uhambile 8. Abantu balambile kakhulu 9. Umntwana uhlakaniphile futhi ufunda kakhulu esikoleni 10. Abafana bakhathele ngoba bagijime kakhulu

(d) 1. The child is injured on his body because he has fallen (wa = fall) from the tree 2. Where have you come from? I come from the doctor 3. They will kill an ox at Khoza's place tomorrow 4. Last year I returned from Johannesburg 5. How does the child write? He writes well 6. With what does he write? He writes with a pencil and pen 7. The boy is good because he studies well at school 8. Dick is drunk today because he drank a lot yesterday 9. Jane, please shut the office now because I want to go, I am in a hurry 10. Mother is glad because the children are clever

110

*Exercise No. 11* (page 65)

(a) 1. Ulambile na? Cha, angilambile  2. UJohn akakhathele kodwa uthukuthele kakhulu  3. Abalungile ngoba baphuza kakhulu  4. Abafana balwile kodwa abalimele  5. Angiboni inja, ngibona ikati  6. Abantwana abathandi iphalishi  7. Awukhulumi isiNgisi kahle kakhulu  8. Abayi edolobheni ngoMgqibelo  9. Ngifuna ikhofi, hhayi itiye, futhi angifuni ushukela  10. UJohn akasebenzi, uthanda ukudlala ibhola, hhayi ukufunda

(b) 1. The children are not clever  2. John is not hungry, he just wants tea  3. Tom drank a lot yesterday but he is not drunk  4. Where is John? I don't know  5. Mother, we don't want to go to school today  6. Mary is not cooking, she is washing clothes  7. The child does not learn English at school  8. I do not work at night, I work only during the day  9. The people do not travel by train on Sunday  10. I like tea, I do not like coffee

(c) 1. Asizufika kusasa  2. Abazuletha imali  3. UJoe akazusebenza kusasa ngoba uyagula  4. Angizutshela wena futhi  5. UTom akasebenzanga izolo futhi akazusebenza namuhla  6. Asizuthenga isinkwa, sizothenga amaswidi kuphela  7. Ubone uTom esitolo na? Cha, angibonanga yena  8. Angifundanga isiZulu esikoleni  9. Angizusiza wena ngoba ngikhathele  10. UJoe akayanga emsebenzini namuhla

(d) 1. We won't come tomorrow, perhaps we will come another time  2. Will you bring meat? No, I will not bring meat, I will only bring bread  3. Mary will not go to town tomorrow because she went to town yesterday  4. Did you learn English at school? No I did not learn English, I only learnt Zulu  5. James has gone but he did not take food  6. We did not see a dog on the path  7. I did not arrive at 8.30, I came early to work  8. The children will not laugh, they will cry  9. Has James returned? No, he hasn't  10. I did not sleep at home last night, I slept at work

(e) 1. Umntwana akekho (lapha) namuhla  2. We Joe, uphi? Ngilapha phandle, angikho endlini  3. Abantu abayanga emsebenzini namuhla, futhi abekho ekhaya  4. Baphi? Angazi  5. Angifuni ukudlala, ngifuna ukusebenza  6. UJoe akathandi ukusebenza ebusuku  7. Asizuzama ukusiza induna  8. Abantwana abazufuna ukufunda, bazofuna ukudlala  9. Awuthandi ukusiza abantu  10. UJoe akathandi ukukhuluma kakhulu

(f) 1. Tom is not at work today  2. Where have the children gone because they are not at school  3. I don't know, perhaps they have gone to the soccer  4. James, where are you? Sir, I am not in the office, I am here outside  5. Mary does not want to shop (buy) today  6. The children do not want to wash in the morning because it is cold  7. You there, child, don't you want to study today? No, teacher, I am sick  8. We don't like to go on foot, we like to go by car  9. I will not try to finish the work today because it is now getting dark, I will come back tomorrow  10. Do the children like to study on Saturday? Some like (to), others do not

*Exercise No. 12* (page 71)

(a) 1. Siza induna uma uthanda  2. Umntwana uyakhala uma elambile  3. Ngiphuza itiye uma ngibuya edolobheni  4. Sidlala ibhola ntambama uma sithanda  5. Asithandi ukusebenza phandle uma lina  6. Uma ulambile cela isinkwa  7. Uma uthisha efika abantwana bayathula  8. UTom uphuza

111

kakhulu ngoLwesihlanu ebusuku uma eholile  9. Uma ubona uJoe esitolo, nika yena imali  10. Angifuni uGumede lapha uma edakiwe

(b) 1. I want you to bring money when you come tomorrow  2. People don't like to work if they are hungry  3. Men, I want you to return to work quickly when you have drawn (your) pay  4. If it rains tomorrow we will not work outside  5. I will go to town if it doesn't rain  6. Children buy sweets when they like  7. People are glad when they get paid  8. Please bring coffee when I come into the office  9. The boys run when they come out of school because they want to play football  10. I like to go on foot when I go to church because it is not far

(c) 1. Ngicabanga ukuthi udokotela ufikile  2. Sithi sithanda ukusebenza lapha  3. Abantwana bathi bafuna amaswidi  4. Uma ubuza yena uzothi uyagula  5. Batheni? Bathe bafuna ukuya ekhaya  6. Uthi uJoe uzofika na? Yebo, ngisho njalo  7. Angicabangi ukuthi bathanda ukusebenza lapha  8. Basho njalo na? Abanye basho njalo  9. Sicela ukuthi siye ekhaya ntambama  10. Ngithanda ukuthi uJoe ashayele imoto ngoba ushayela kahle  11. UTom ufisa ukuthola umsebenzi ngonyaka ozayo ngoba ufuna imali  12. Abafana bafuna ngidlale ibhola nabo

(d) 1. The person says he is hungry, he also wants money  2. Does he say that? Where does he come from?  3. He says he comes from home at Ndwedwe  4. Tell him to come inside, I want to talk to him  5. The children hope that the teacher will come with sweets to school tomorrow  6. Sir, I wish to speak to Albert. Is he here?  7. No, he has gone, he says he will be back this afternoon  8. Where has he gone? I think he has gone to the doctor because he is sick  9. Jane, we request (please) bring the money tomorrow  10. When you go into the office what will you request of the boss? I will ask to go home at the end of the month.

*Exercise No. 13*  (page 81)

(a) 1. Inja iphuza amanzi  2. Induna ibiza abantu  3. Izinkomo ziphi?  4. Izingane zikhalelani? Zilambile  5. Abafana bafuna ukushaya inja. Inja kabani? Inja yami  6. Imoto yami ihamba kahle  7. Abantwana badlala phandle. Abantwana bakabani? Abantwana bakhe  8. Nika ingane ubisi uma ikhala kakhulu  9. Musa ukudlala nezinyoka ngoba ziluma abantu  10. Abantwana bakho badlala engadini yami

(b) 1. Where is the dog now? I don't know, it has run away  2. The man wants to work here  3. The cattle are eating grass on the hill  4. The dogs bit children yesterday  5. The headmen will come with the people to the chief  6. The girl wants to work in the factory  7. Why is the baby crying? It is crying because it wants milk  8. Where are my goats? They have gone to the river  9. People eat meat but cattle do not eat meat, they eat grass  10. Where is your child? He has gone to school

(c) 1. Indoda ayisebenzi ehhovisi, isebenza egalaji  2. Izinja zami azilumi  3. Izinkomo zakhe zilapha, aziyangi emfuleni  4. Izinkukhu zabo azilungile, zibanga umsindo  5. Ingane ayifuni ukuphuza ubisi, ayilambile  6. Izinja zami azithandi ukuluma, zifuna ukudlala nje  7. Izimbuzi zilambile na? Cha, kodwa zifuna amanzi  8. Inkosi ayifuni ukukhuluma nabantu namuhla  9.

Indoda ayisebenzi kahle, mhlawumbe ikhathele 10. Cha, ayikhathele, idakiwe

(d) 1. My car is not in the garage, where is it? 2. Your belongings are on the table, they are not in the cupboard 3. The bird does not like meat, it wants bread 4. We are glad because the snake is not in the garden, it has gone 5. The babies are not good because they do not want to sleep at night 6. The girl does not like coffee, she drinks only tea 7. People do not eat grass but cattle eat grass 8. Goats don't eat meat but people like meat very much 9. The goats are not in the garden, there are only dogs 10. Your dogs are no good because they bite

*Exercise No. 14* (page 84)

(a) 1. Izinkomo ziwu/zingu 12 2. Abantu bangu/bawu 23 3. Abantwana bami bawu/bangu 3, abantwana bakho bangu/bawu 5 4. Ngizoletha imali kusasa. Uzoletha malini? Ngizoletha amarandi awu 15 5. Umntwana ucela amasenti angu 75 6. Ngizothengisa imoto yami ngamarandi awu 2 000 7. Izolo ngithenge izingubo edolobheni, zishibhile edolobheni kodwa zidulile ekhaya 8. Izimbuzi zakho zibiza malini? Zibiza amarandi awu 45 9. UJoe uhola malini? Uhola amarandi angu 90 ngesonto 10. Ubhanana ubiza malini? Ubiza amasenti awu 90 idazini. Kudulile kakhulu lokho. Kulungile, ngizodayisa ngamasenti awu 75

(b) 1. The people on the bus are 45 2. My cattle at home are 11 3. Tomorrow I will get paid, I will get R85 4. I paid R3 000 for my car 5. Father is selling goats for R65 6. I like to buy clothes in Durban because they are cheap there 7. Hey, boy, what are you selling? I am selling matungulus. How much do you want? I want 50 cents 8. The boys want to play football but James has not come, they are only 10 9. How much does Mary earn? She earns a lot, she gets R500 per month 10. When I have sold my fowls I will buy your goat for R40

*Exercise No. 15* (page 90)

(a) 1. Sinesinkwa nenyama 2. Unemali na? 3. Indoda inenduku/iphethe induku 4. UMary unabantwana ekhaya, bangu 3 5. Ngafika kaningi ngenyanga edlule 6. Abantwana bacula kamnandi esontweni 7. Inja iluma kakhulu 8. Sinezinkukhu ekhaya, zimhlophe 9. Abantwana baningi esikoleni, abanye bakhulu, abanye bancane 10. UJane uzogeza izingubo ngoba zingcolile

(b) 1. Say, Tom where are you going? I am going to the shop 2. Have you got money? Yes, I have money on me 3. How much have you got? I have R2 4. Some children learn easily, others learn with difficulty 5. The teacher is in the habit of hitting us children with a ruler on the body, he only hits three times 6. The dog is black but the goats are red 7. Mother has a garden at home, she likes very much to work in her garden 8. Has your father got a car? Yes, he has a car 9. What is his car like? It is white 10. The people have work, they travel to their work by bus

(c) 1. Kushisa kakhulu kwaZulu 2. UTom uyagula. Kunjalo na? Yebo, kunjalo 3. Kukhona izinja ejalidini na? 4. Kuhle ukusebenza, akukuhle ukulova 5. Akululula ukukhuluma isiZulu kahle kodwa siyazama 6. Kukhona

113

ukudla endlini  7. Abantu bonke baye emsebenzini  8. Indoda ayifuni ukudla, ifuna imali kuphela nje  9. Ngihamba ngebhasi kuphela, angihambi ngesitimela  10. Izinkukhu zishibhile, zibiza amarandi awu 4 kuphela

(d)  1. It is easy to ride a bicycle but it is not easy to drive a car  2. Thoko, have you passed? Yes, I have passed. That is very good  3. Beware, there is a snake in the garden  4. Teacher wants all the children to come tomorrow  5. David does not work, he just loafs  6. All the cattle have gone to the river, they want water  7. The boy is not good because he has taken all the money  8. Foreman, we have finished the work. Allright, you may go then  9. The boys do not want to study at school, they only like to play  10. I have money today because yesterday I got pay

*Exercise No. 16*  (page 95)
(a)  1. Bantwana, musani ukubanga/ukwenza umsindo  2. Mntanami, ngicela wenze itiye manje  3. Wazini yena? Akazi lutho  4. Lo mfana/umfana lo ufunda kahle esikoleni kodwa lowo mfana/umfana lowo akafundi, uyaganga nje  5. Ngifuna ukuthenga lezo zinkukhu/izinkukhu lezo: zimalini/zibiza malini?  6. Imali yami iphi? Nansi/nayi  7. Umfana ufike izolo, nangu phandle futhi, uthi ufuna ukuthenga umango  8. Abantu baphi namuhla? Nampa/naba, balinde phandle  9. Le mbuzi/Imbuzi le imhlophe kodwa leyo mbuzi/imbuzi leyo imnyama  10. Izinja zenzani? Nazi, ziyadlala nje, azilumi

(b)  1. You men, what are you doing now? Sir, we are working, we are making tables  2. This person knows everything but that one knows nothing (does not know anything)  3. The dog knows the girl but it will bite other people  4. These children study well at school  5. Do you want to buy these fowls or those?  6. I want these, how much do they cost?  7. Take this (thing) and go, tomorrow you will get something else  8. Here are people outside, they say they are hungry  9. Here are the fowls, they are eating blackjacks in the garden  10. I want you to speak nicely, I don't like to hear that

(c)  1. UPhyllis uyakwazi ukufunda kahle  2. Lo mntwana uyakwazi ukugijima ngokushesha  3. UJoseph akakwazi ukuhlamba kodwa abanye abafana bayakwazi  4. Uthisha ufanele ukusiza abantwana  5. Ufanele ukuhamba manje ngoba umsebenzi uqedile  6. Sifanele ukusebenza kusasa na? Yebo, kufanele  7. Umntwana ufanele ukuthula uma abazali bakhe bekhuluma  8. Mary, awufanele ukugeza izingubo ngoba azingcolile  9. Abantwana bafanele ukubanga umsindo kanje? Cha, akufanele  10. Angikwazi ukukhuluma isiXhosa kodwa ngiyakwazi ukukhuluma isiZulu

(d)  1. Can you drive a car?  2. Joseph cannot speak English  3. We know (how) to ride a bicycle  4. If they go at 6 they ought to return at 12  5. The child should not drink lemonade, he should only drink milk  6. You must work well at school, not fool around  7. I can use a machine but Peter cannot  8. A person ought not to drive a car if he has been drinking  9. Men, you must go now and come back tomorrow if it does not rain  10. Teacher here is a boy outside, he has come many times, he says he wants to join the school

114

# ANSWERS TO ADDITIONAL READING AND EXERCISES

## 1. Joseph Gumede

Joseph Gumede stays at Umlazi and works in a factory in Durban. He gets up at 5 a.m. but not every day because sometimes he works at night. He likes very much to work at night, he says he gets extra pay, also he gets time during the day to buy things at the shop. To go to work he travels by bus or by train, sometimes he goes by taxi. He himself is paid by the week but others get paid by the month. At work they get tea and bread when they begin work, they also drink tea at 10 o'clock. They eat lunch at 12.30 and knock off at 5. He arrives home at 7.

(a) Uhlala eMlazi, usebenza efektri eThekwini.
(b) Uvuka ngo 5.
(c) Cha, akavuki ekuseni zonke izinsuku.
(d) Uthi uhola kahle futhi uyakwazi ukuthenga esitolo emini.
(e) Uhamba ngebhasi noma ngesitimela noma ngetekisi.
(f) Uhola ngesonto.
(g) Badla isinkwa netiye.
(h) Badla ilantshi ngo 12.30.
(i) Ushayisa ngo 5.
(j) Ufika ekhaya ngo 7.

## 2. Ingadi yethu

Sinengadi ekhaya eNdwedwe. Umama uthanda ingadi yethu kakhulu, usebenza khona zonke izinsuku. Uvuka ekuseni alungise ibhulakufesi ngoba singena esikoleni ngo-pasi seven. Sonke siya esikoleni ngezinyawo ngoba kuseduze. Emva kwalokho umama usebenza engadini. Utshala imifino nezimbali nezithelo. Ngesinye isikhathi uthengisa izithelo namaqanda.

Ekhaya sinezinkukhu nezimbuzi kodwa umama uthukuthela kakhulu uma zingena engadini ngoba zenza umonakalo khona, izinkukhu ziphanda phansi nezimbuzi zidla imifino.

NgoMgqibelo ngisiza umama engadini. Udadewethu uDudu uyasiza kodwa yena uthanda kakhulu ukusebenza endlini, uthanda ukubhaka amakhekhe futhi upheka itiye noma ikhofi. Umama uphuza kakhulu itiye kodwa mina ngithanda ikhofi. UDudu uphuza iCoke kuphela.

## 3. Shopping trip

Tomorrow we will get up at 5 because we want to go to town, we want to buy at the shops. We will go by bus because we want to arrive in town early. The people in the bus are many, they all go to town on Saturdays, they want to buy at the shops because things are cheap there. Some will buy food, others will buy clothes, others meat, others beer and spirits. As for me, I will not buy food, I only want shoes. My brother will buy a hat. Father doesn't want to buy anything, he says he will just look because he has no money. Mother wants meat and potatoes and sugar and rice. My sister wants to buy a record. The shops will close at 1 and then we return home, we will return by train because it is cheap on the train. At home we will have some tea and then go to the soccer.

(a) Sizoya edolobheni.
(b) Ngoba sifuna ukufika ekuseni edolobheni.
(c) Bazothenga ukudla noma izingubo noma inyama noma utshwala nogologo.
(d) Ngizothenga izicathulo mina.
    Umfowethu uzothenga isigqoko.
(e) Ubaba akazuthenga lutho.
(f) Izitolo zivala ngo 1.
(g) Sihamba ngesitimela, ngoba kushibhile.
(h) Ntambama sizoya ebholeni.


## 4. James, Velaphi and Themba

JAMES:  Sawubona, Velaphi, unjani?
VELAPHI:  Yebo, sawubona James. Ngiyaphila. Unjani wena?
JAMES:  Nami ngikhona.
    (Themba now comes into sight)
    Nangu uThemba
THEMBA:  Sanibona bangane. Ninjani?
J & V:  Yebo, sawubona Themba. Sisaphila. Unjani wena?
THEMBA:  Ngilungile. Niyaphi nina?
JAMES:  Sizothenga esitolo bese siya eposini ngoba uVelaphi ufuna ukushaya ucingo.
THEMBA:  Nami ngizoshaya ucingo ngifuna ukutshela umfowethu ukuthi ngizofika kuyena eGoli ngoMsombuluko. Ngizohamba ngesitimela. Niyazi ukuthi ngizosebenza eGoli na?
VELAPHI:  Siyajabula ukuzwa lokhu. Siya eThekwini thina, ngithole umsebenzi egalaji eJacobs ngizoqala ngoLwesibili. UJames naye uthemba ukuthi uzothola umsebenzi eThekwini.
JAMES:  Kunjalo. Umfowethu uDick usebenza efektri eMobeni uthi ngifanele ukufika masinyane mhlawumbe ngizothola umsebenzi.
THEMBA:  Kuhle kakhulu lokho. Ngiyethemba ukuthi konke kuzohamba kahle. Salani kahle bangane bami.
J & V:  Yebo hamba kahle Themba, ufike kahle eGoli.

# Appendix II

## ALTERNATIVE WAYS OF EXPRESSING IDEAS

As stated in the Preface, where there are alternative methods of expressing an idea, only one way — the easiest — has been used in this Course. However, in order to assist students to understand Zulu speakers who may be using the alternative methods of expression, certain of these alternatives are set out in this Appendix. The paragraph references are to the same topic in the Manual.

► 1. *Paragraph 9* Question: Why? (Negative Why not?)
You do not use -elani to form the negative of Why, but make a normal negative statement followed by Ngani.
Why do you not like tea? = You do not like tea followed by ngani = Awuthandi itiye ngani? or Awuthandi ngani itiye?
Why are they not working? = They are not working, plus ngani = Abasebenzi ngani?

► 2. *Paragraph 15* Negative instruction
In addition to Musa/Musani uku . . . you can say: unga/ninga . . . with the verb ending in an -i:

| | |
|---|---|
| Don't go now (to one person) | Ungahambi manje |
| Don't go now (to more than one) | Ningahambi manje |
| Joyce, don't open the door | Joyce, ungavuli umnyango |

► 3. *Paragraph 17* Health queries
If somebody says he is not well, you may wish to ask:

| | |
|---|---|
| What is the matter? | Unani? or Uphethwe yini? |
| In reply: I have a headache | Ngiphethwe yikhanda |
| I have a cold or fever | Ngiphethwe ngumkhuhlane |
| I have a stomach ache | Ngiphethwe yisisu |
| I am sorry to hear that | Ngiyadabuka ukuzwa lokho |

► 4. *Paragraph 18* The word 'Please'
In addition to ngicela u . . . you can say: ake u . . . with the verb similarly ending in an -e:
Please shut the door   Ake uvale umnyango
Mary, please bring the tea now   Mary, ake ulethe itiye manje

► 5. *Paragraph 22* To express the object
Besides the Emphatic Pronouns mina, wena, etc it is common to hear Objective Concords being used. These come immediately in front of the verb and are the same as the ordinary (subjective) concords except where they are single letters: U (you) becomes KU and U (he/she) becomes M
He is calling me   Instead of: Ubiza mina   you could have:
He does me call   U ya ngi biza = Uyangibiza
Where is Joe? UJoe uphi? They want him   Instead of: Bafuna

yena  you could have: Ba ya m funa = Bayamfuna

I want to help you = I want to you help  Ngifuna uku ku siza = Ngifuna ukukusiza

They will tell us tomorrow = They will us tell tomorrow:
Ba zo si tshela kusasa = Bazositshela kusasa

Are the children here? I saw them in the shop this morning = I them saw = Abantwana bakhona na? Ngi ba bone esitolo = Ngibabone esitolo ekuseni

Gumede is outside but I do not want him = I do not him want
UGumede uphandle kodwa angi m funi = angimfuni

To assist in remembering this type of speech, think of the word used in greeting: Sawubona or Sakubona which is a contraction of si ya ku bona — we do you see — we see you

6.  *Paragraph 44*  If/When in the Negative
Use UMA followed by the concord plus -NGA- plus verb ending in -I
Examples:
If we return    Uma sibuya
If we do not return    Uma singabuyi
If you work tomorrow    Uma usebenza kusasa
If you do not work tomorrow    Uma ungasebenzi kusasa

7.  *Paragraph 45/46*  More uses of UKUTHI
Questions such as: 'Do you know where/when/who/how/what etc' must incorporate the words -yazi ukuthi (i.e. know *that*) followed by the question itself. Examples: Do you know where Joe works? = Do you know that: Joe he works where? = Uyazi ukuthi uJoe usebenzaphi? Do you know when Mary will return? = Do you know that: Mary will return when? Uyazi ukuthi uMary uzobuya nini?
The replies would be:
Positive:   Yebo, ngiyazi ukuthi uJoe usebenzaphi
Negative:   Angazi ukuthi uJoe usebenzaphi

8.  *Paragraph 47 & 52*  Three more noun classes (and their negatives)
There are 3 more classes of nouns fairly often in use:

*Ummy Class*   Begin with UM- but do not refer to people
        Prefixes: Singular  Um-    Plural  Imi -
        Concords: Sing. u-  (negative awu-)  Plural i-  (negative ayi-)
The tree/trees need water    Umuthi udinga/imithi idinga amanzi
The tree/trees do not need water    Umuthi awudingi/imithi ayidingi amanzi

*Issy Class*   Begin with ISI-
        Prefixes: Singular Isi-    Plural Izi-
        Concords: Sing. si-  (negative  asi-)  Plural zi-  (negative azi-)
The animal is/is not drinking    Isilwane siyaphuza/isilwane asiphuzi
The animals are/are not drinking    Izilwane ziyaphuza/aziphuzi

*Illy Class* If a noun commences with I- but is not followed by M or N (the I'm In class) or SI (the Issy class) it is in this class (with a few exceptions)

Prefixes: Singular I-, Ili-  Plural Ama-

Concords: Sing. li-  (negative ali-) Plural a-  (negative awa-)

The cat is/is not catching a rat  Ikati libamba/alibambi igundane

The cats are/are not catching rats  Amakati abamba/awabambi amagundane

The reason for the unusual concord LI- is that the prefix was originally Ili- but when they contracted it to I- they retained LI- as the concord.

▶ 9.  *Paragraph 51* Whose? Kabani?

If the owner is a person in the sub-class of You People, such as ubaba, ugogo, udokotela, uthisha, uGumede (or any name) you must use KA and drop the initial u-.

Father's car  Imoto kababa

Whose money?  Khumalo's money  Imali kabani?  Imali kaKhumalo

The doctor's children  Abantwana bakadokotela

10.  *Paragraph 57* Adjectives used the 'other way'

If you wish to use an adjective in the English idiom as coming before the noun e.g. *the red car* instead of *the car is red*, in Zulu you still put the noun first but use the link word 'who/which', i.e. *the car which is red*. There are difficulties in adapting certain of the concords but the general rule is:

If the noun begins in an  i-  the link is  e-

If the noun begins in a  u-  the link is  o-

If the noun begins in an  a-  the link is  a-

*Examples:*

The person is suitable  Umuntu ulungile
A suitable person  Umuntu olungile

The car is dirty  Imoto ingcolile
A dirty car  Imoto engcolile

The people are many  Abantu baningi
Many people  Abantu abaningi

▶ 11.  *Paragraph 64* Can, May

Use NGA between concord and verb

You can go now = you may go now  Ungahamba manje

We can return tomorrow  Singabuya kusasa

Mary, you can bring the tea (this is very near to: Please bring)

Mary, ungaletha itiye

▶ 12.  *Paragraph 65* Come: alternative to Fika

It is common to hear them use the word -ZA in some form or other

The people are coming  Abantu bayeza

Is the doctor coming?  Udokotela uyeza na?

No, he is not coming today  Cha, akezi namuhla

119

# ENGLISH — ZULU VOCABULARY
## (words used in this course)

The figure shown in italics refers to the paragraph in which the word/construction will be found

Abbreviations used:

| | | |
|---|---|---|
| aux — auxiliary | loc — locative | pl — plural |
| conc — concord | neg — negative | pron — pronoun |
| conj — conjunction | n — noun | vb — verb |

\* denotes the word appears in the Addendum on page 124

### A

able, be   conc + yakwazi uku-  *63*
above   phezulu
accident   ingozi (pl) izingozi
accompany   hamba na-  *31*
aeroplane   ibhanoyi
affair   indaba (pl) izindaba
after   emuva
afternoon   ntambama
again   futhi, kabili
again, do   phinda
ago, long   kade
agree   vuma
air   umoya
alive, be   phila  *17*
all   -onke  *59*
all right   -lungile  *57*
all right, it's   kulungile  *58*
all together   kanyekanye  *56*
also   futhi  *6*
alternative   hhayi  *20*
am (aux) not expressed
and (conj)   futhi  *6*
and (with)   na- + fusion  *30*
and not   hhayi  *20*
and then   bese  *14*
angry, be   thukuthele  *39*
\*any (quantity) not expressed
anything   lutho
\*appear   vela
approach   sondela
appropriate, be   kufanele  *64*
are (verb 'to be') not expressed
are (number)   (conc) + ngu/wu  *53*
arise   vuka
around, be   khona  *11*
arrive   fika
as for, as regards   mina, wena etc.  *21*
as well (also)   futhi  *6*
      (and, too)   na-  *30*
ask (enquire)   buza
ask for (request)   cela
assent given   kulungile  *58*
      kufanele  *64*

assumed, I (an excuse)   bengithi  *45*
at (place) locative  *35*
at (time)   ngo-  *33*
at all, not   neze
at the place of   kwa  *36*
at the time that   see 'when'
available, be   khona  *11*
away from (place)   (loc)  *35*
away, come   phuma
away, go   suka
away, run   baleka
away, take   susa
axe   imbazo (pl) izimbazo

### B

baby   ingane (pl) izingane
bad   a + (conc) + lungile  *57*
badly   kabi
bananas   ubhanana
bank to, from   ebhange
basket   ubhasikidi
beans   ubhontshisi
beast   inkomo (pl) izinkomo
because   ngoba  *6, 9*
beer   utshwala
beg   cela
begin   qala
behind   emuva
bell   insimbi
belongings   impahla
below   phansi
better   -ngcono  *59*
beware   qaphela, bhasopha
bicycle   ibhayisikili
bird   inyoni (pl) izinyoni
bit, not a!   neze!
bite   luma
black   mnyama  *57*
boss   umnumzana, ubasi
boy   umfana (pl) abafana
bread   isinkwa

bring  letha
bring back  buyisa
brother, my  umfowethu (pl) abafowethu
brother, your  umfowenu (pl) abafowenu
bucket  ibhakede
bus  ibhasi
but  kodwa  6
but not  hhayi  20
buy  thenga
by (place)  (loc)  35
by (per)  nga-  33
by means of  nga-  33

## C

call  biza
can  yakwazi uku-  63;  nga-11 App II
cannot  a + (conc) + kwazi uku-  63
car  imoto
care, I don't!  anginandaba!
carefully  kahle  56
cat  ikati  (pl) amakati
cattle  izinkomo
cease (doing)  yeka  68
cent  isenti (pl) amasenti  54
cheap  -shibhile  54
cheque  isheke (pl) amasheke
chief  inkosi (pl) amakhosi
child  umntwana (pl) abantwana
church, at, to, in, from  esontweni
clean, make  sula
clever  -hlakaniphile  39
close (shut)  vala
cloth  indwangu (pl) izindwangu
clothes  izingubo
coffee  ikhofi
cold, be  banda  29
cold  -makhaza  29, 58
come  fika, -za  12 App II
come here!  woza lapha!
come away  phuma, suka
come back  buya
come in  ngena
come near  sondela
come out  phuma
complain  khala
complete  qeda
condition, what?  -njani?  57
cook  pheka
cool, be  -pholile  29
correct  -lungile  57
cost  biza  54
cross  -thukuthele  39
cry  khala
cupboard  ikhabede
cut  sika

## D

danger  ingozi
daughter  indodakazi (pl) amadodakazi
daughter of house  inkosazana  18
day  ilanga  29
day, during  emini
dead  -file  39
dear  -dulile  54
deliver goods  diliva
depart  suka
desire  fisa, thanda, funa  46
desist  yeka  68  musa  15
did (aux past) not expressed
die  fa  65
difficult  -nzima  -lukhuni  58
dig  mba  65
dirty  -ngcolile  57
disapproval  akufanele  64
discharge  xosha
dishes  izitsha
dismiss  xosha
do (present aux) not expressed
do (make)  enza  60
doctor  udokotela
dog  inja (pl) izinja
don't!  musa  15  hayibo  20
*don't (neg. action)  a + (neg.)  40
door  umnyango
down  phansi
dozen  idazini
drink  phuza
drive (car)  shayela
drunk  -dakiwe  39
Durban, to, from, at, in  eThekwini
during  nga-  33

## E

early  ekuseni
earn  hola
easy  -lula  56, 58
eat  dla  65
elephant  indlovu (pl) izindlovu
employment  umsebenzi
end of month  ekupheleni kwenyanga  23
English  isiNgisi
enquire  buza
enter  ngena
every day  zonke izinsuku
excuse me!  uxolo  18
expensive  -dulile  54
extra  ngaphezulu

## F

fall  wa
Fanakalo (instances)  2, 4, 20, 21
far  kude
farewell, say  valelisa  17

121

farewell! sala/hamba kahle *17*
fast ngokushesha
father ubaba
fetch landa
fill up gcwalisa
find thola
finish qeda
finish (stop work) shayisa, qeda
fish inhlanzi (pl) izinhlanzi
five -hlanu *53*
flower imbali (pl) izimbali
food ukudla
fool around ganga
foot, on go hamba phansi, ngezinyawo
football ibhola
for (buy, sell) nga- *54*
forget khohlwa
four -ne *53*
fowl inkukhu (pl) izinkukhu
Friday uLwesihlanu *23*
friend umngane (pl) abangane
from (place) (loc) *35*

G
garden ingadi
game umdlalo
gentleman umnumzana (pl) abanumzana
get thola
get paid hola
get up (wake) vuka
girl intombazana
give nika
glad, be jabula
go hamba
go to ya *19*
goat imbuzi (pl) izimbuzi
good -lungile *39, 58*
goods impahla
goodbye sala/hamba kahle *17*
goodbye, say valelisa *17*
good-morning sawubona/sakubona *17*
got (be in possession) not expressed *55*
gradually kancane *56*
grandmother ugogo
grasss utshani
grateful, be bonga *17*
greatly kakhulu *56*
greet, to bingelela *17*
greeting (general) sawubona *17*

H
hammer isando
hand isandla
happy, be jabula
hard -lukhuni, -nzima *57, 58*
hard, work kakhulu, kanzima *56*

has/have (recent past action) Past Tense *25*
has/have (possess) phethe, na- *55*
he (stressed) yena *21*
head ikhanda
head of family umnumzana *17*
headman induna (pl) izinduna
hear zwa *65*
heavens izulu *29*
heavy -nzima *57*
help siza
her/hers (adj) -akhe *50*
her (object) yena *22*, -m- 5 App II
herself yena *21*
here lapha
here, be khona *11*
here is/are nangu etc. *62*
hill intaba (pl) izintaba
him (object) yena *22*, -m- 5 App II
himself yena *21*
his -akhe *50*
hit shaya
hold on (telephone) yima *68*
home, at, to, from ekhaya *35*
hope themba *46*
hospital, in, to, at esibhedlela *35*
hot, be shisa, balela *29*
house indlu (pl) izindlu
how: what manner? kanjani? *38*
      what condition? -njani? *57*
      what means? ngani? *34*
how come? kwenzenjani? *66*
how do you say (in Zulu) kuthiwani ngesiZulu?
how many? -ngaki? *57*
how much? malini? *54*
how often? kangaki? *56*
how old? neminyaka emingaki? *18*
hungry -lambile *39*
hurry shesha
hurry, be in a -jahile *39*
hurt -limele *39*
husband indoda, umyeni
hut indlu (pl) izindlu

I
I (stressed) mina *21*
I say! we *12*
I say (you must) -bo *12*
if uma *44*
if not see item 6 Appendix II Page 118
ill, be gula
immediately manjemanje, khona manje
in (place) (loc) *35*
in order -lungile *57*
indeed impela
infant ingane (pl) izingane
injured -limele *39*
inside phakathi

122

instruct tshela *46*
into (loc) *35*
iron (vb) ayina
   (metal) insimbi (pl) izinsimbi
it (I'm In class) i- *48*
it does not matter akunandaba
it, it is (indefinite) ku- *58*
it is so! kunjalo! *58*
it is not so! akunjalo! *58*
it's all right kulungile *58*
it's not all right akulungile *58*


J
job umsebenzi
Johannesburg iGoli *37*
just (only) nje, kuphela *59*


K
kill bulala
king inkosi
kitchen, in ekhishini *35*
knife umese
knock-off (work) shayisa
know azi *60*


L
lady inkosikazi
lady, young intombazana, inkosazana
last week isonto eledlule *23*
last month inyanga edlule *23*
last year unyaka odlule *23*
late, be phuza ukufika, fika emuva
laugh hleka
learn funda
leave shiya
leave (depart) suka, phuma
leave off yeka
letter incwadi (pl) izincwadi
lie down lala
lies, tell qamba amanga
light (easy) -lula *57, 58*
like thanda
like this kanje *56*
like that kanjalo
like how? kanjani? *56*
liquor ugologo
little -ncane *57*
little, a kancane *56*
listen lalela
loaf (idle) lova
long ago kade
look at buka
look for funa
look out! qaphela, bhasopha!
lot, a kakhulu *56*
love thanda

M
machine umshini
madam inkosikazi, inkosazana, umedemu
maid (domestic) intombazana
make enza *60*
make a noise banga umsindo
man indoda (pl) amadoda
manner, in this kanje *56*
manner, in that kanjalo
manner, in what? kanjani? *56*
manner (by means of) nga- *33*
many -ningi *57*
many times kaningi *56*
master umnumzana (pl) abanumzana
matter (affair) indaba (pl) izindaba
matter, what's the kwenzenjani *66*
matter, it does not akunandaba
*may I? ngicela
me (object) mina *22*, ngi- *5* App II
mealie-meal impuphu
means, by m. of nga- *33*
means, by what? ngani? *34*
meat inyama
medicine umuthi
meet again bonana *17*
merely nje, kuphela *59*
midday emini
milk ubisi
mine -ami *50*
minister umfundisi (pl) abafundisi
miss inkosazana
mistakes amaphutha *17*
mistress inkosikazi, umedemu
Monday uMsombuluko *23*
money imali
money values: cents amasenti, awu/angu- *54*
              rands amarandi, awu-/angu *54*
month inyanga *23*
month, this ngalenyanga *23*
month, last ngenyanga edlule *23*
month, next ngenyanga ezayo *23*
moon inyanga
more futhi
morning ekuseni
mother umama
motorbike isithuthuthu
motorcar imoto (pl) izimoto
mountain intaba (pl) izintaba
much (a lot) kakhulu *56*
much, how? malini? *54*
must (command) -bo- *12*
must (should) fanele uku- *64*
my ami *50*
myself mina *21*

123

## N

name igama *17*
naughty, be ganga
near, nearby eduze
near, come sondela *17*
necessary, be kufanele *64*
need dinga
never! neze, hhayikhona *20*
next week ngesonto elizayo *23*
next month ngenyanga ezayo *23*
next year ngonyaka ozayo *23*
nice -mnandi *56, 57*
nicely kahle *56*
night, at ebusuku
no cha *5*
no! hhayikhona! *20*
no good (bad) a + (conc) + lungile *57*
no good, that's akulungile lokho *58*
no matter akulutho, akunandaba
no such thing! akukho lokho *58*
noise umsindo
not (alternative) hhayi *20*
not: negative action *40–42*
not: negative condition *40*
not: negative place *43*
not at all, not a bit neze
not here (absent) a + (conc) + kho *43*
not now! hhayi manje *20*
not so! akunjalo *58*
nothing lutho
now manje
nurse unesi

## O

*obey lalela
office ihhovisi (loc. ehhovisi)
*often kaningi *56*
OK, it's kulungile *58*
old, how? neminyaka emingaki *17*
on (place) locative *35*
on (day) ngo- *33*
on foot, go hamba phansi, ngezinyawo
one -nye *53*
once kanye *56*
only kuphela, nje *59*
open vula
opinion, give thi *45*
or noma *6*
order, be in -lungile *57*
other (people) abanye abantu
ought to fanele uku- *64*
our -ethu *50*
ourselves thina *21*
out of (place) locative *35*
out, come/go phuma
out, look! qaphela, bhasopha
outside phandle

over (on top) phezulu
over (again) futhi
over there lapho
overcast, be kusithibele *29*
overseer induna
ox inkabi (pl) izinkabi

## P

parent umzali (pl) abazali
parcel impahla
pardon! nxephe, uxolo *17*
past (time of clock) pasi *23*
path indlela (pl) izindlela
pencil ipensele
people abantu
per nga- *33*
perhaps mhlawumbe
person umuntu (pl) abantu
paid, be hola
*pay khokha
pig ingulube (pl) izingulube
place (noun) indawo (pl) izindawo
place (put) beka
place (at place of) kwa- *36*
place to . . . indawo yoku- *67*
play dlala
play the fool ganga
pleasant -mnandi *57*
please ngicela *13*, ake u- *4* App II
pleased, be jabula *17*
porridge iphalishi
possess phethe, (conc) + na- *55*
post office to, at, from eposini
potatoes amazambane
practise zijwayeza *17*
premises, on the ejalidini
prepare lungisa
present, be khona *11*
price, what? malini? *54*
purse isikhwama
put beka
put inside faka

## Q

queen inkosikazi
quickly ngokushesha
quick, be shesha
quiet, be thula

## R

rain (noun) imvula
rain (verb) -na *29*
rake ireki
rand irandi (pl) amarandi *54*
*read funda
red -bomvu *57*

rejoice  jabula
remove  susa
repeat  phinda
request  cela
required, it is  kufanele  64
rest  phumula
return  buya
return from  buya + (loc)
return to  buyela/phindela + (loc)
ride  gibela
right, be  qinisile
ring bell  shaya insimbi
room  ikamelo
rope  intambo, indophi
run  gijima
run away  baleka

S
*Saturday, on  noMgqibelo  23
say  thi  45
say, I!  we  12
say so  sho njalo  45
school at, to, from, in  esikoleni
see  bona
sell  thengisa, dayisa  54
she (stressed)  yena  21
sheep  imvu (pl) izimvu
shoes  izicathulo
shop, at, to, from, in  esitolo  35
should  fanele uku-  64
show  khombisa
shut  vala
sick, be  gula
silent, be  thula
sir  mnumzana
sit  hlala
six  isithupha  53
sky  izulu  29
sleep  lala
slowly  kancane  56, ngokungasheshi  17
small  -ncane  57
smoke  bhema
snake  inyoka (pl) izinyoka
so (thus)  njalo  45
soccer  ibhola
softly  kahle, kancane  56
some (quantity) not expressed
some people  abanye abantu
sometimes  ngesinye isikhathi
son  indodana (pl) amadodana
*son of the house  inkosana  17
soon  masinyane
sorry!  nxephe  17
sorry, I am (sympathy)  ngiyadabuka  17
sorry, I am (wrongful act)  ngiyaxolisa  17
sort, this  -nje  58
sort, that  -njalo  58

sort, what?  -njani?  57
speak  khuluma
spear  umkhonto
stand  ma  65
stand still!  yima!  68
start  qala
stay (live)  hlala
stay (remain)  sala  17
steal  ntshontsha
stick  induku (pl) izinduku
stone  itshe
stop (action)  yeka uku-  68
stop! (stand)  yima!  63
stop that!  hayibo!  20
store  see 'shop'
stove  isitofu
string  intambo
study  funda
such thing, there is  kukhona  58
such thing, there is no  akukho  58
*sugar  ushukela
suitable  -lungile  39, 57
summer  ehlobo
sun  ilanga
Sunday, on  ngeSonto  23
surname  isibongo  17
sweep  shanela
sweet  -mnandi  56, 57
sweets  amaswidi
swim  hlamba

T
table  itafula
take  thatha
take away  susa
take out  khipha
talk  khuluma
taxi  itekisi
tea  itiye
teacher  uthishela
tearoom, to, from, at  ethilomu  35
tell  tshela
thank you  ngiyabonga  17
that (demonstrative)  61
that (thing, idea)  lokho  61
that is so/right  kunjalo  58
that is not so  akunjalo  58
that's good  kuhle lokho
that's no good  akulungile lokho  58
their  -abo  50
them (object)  bona  22,  ba- 5 App II
themselves  bona  21
then, and  bese  14
then, well  pho, pho-ke
there  lapho
there, be  khona  11
there is  kukhona  58

125

there is not   akukho   *58*
thereafter   bese   *14*
these (demonstrative)   *61*
they (people)   ba-
they (I'm In class)   zi-
thing   into (pl) izinto
think   cabanga, thi   *45*
think so   sho njalo   *45*
this (demonstrative)   *61*
this (indefinite)   lokhu   *61*
this week   ngalelisonto   *23*
this month   ngalenyanga   *23*
this year   ngalonyaka   *23*
those (demonstrative)   *61*
thought, I (an excuse)   bengithi
three   -thathu   *53*
thunder   duma   *29*
Thursday   uLwesine   *23*
tie   bopha
time   isikhathi
time, all the   sonke isikhathi, njalo
time, there is no!   asikho isikhathi   *67*
time to (+ action)   isikhathi soku-   *67*
time, what's the?   sikhathi sini?   *45*
tired   -khathele   *39*
to (place)   (loc)   *35*
to (infinitive)   uku-   *7*
to, talk   khuluma na-   *31*
tobacco   ugwayi
today   namuhla, namhlanje
together, all   kanyekanye
togt   itoho
tomorrow   kusasa
too (also)   futhi
too (as well as)   na-   *32*
top, on   phezulu
towards   (loc)   *35*
train   isitimela
translate   humusha
travel   hamba   *19*
travel to   ya   *19*
*true, it is   impela
try   zama
Tuesday   uLwesibili   *23*
twice   kabili   *56*
two   -bili   *53*

U
underneath   phansi
understand   zwa, qonda
us (object)   thina   *22*,   si- 5 App II
use   sebenzisa
used to (habit)   vama uku-
used to (past) Remote Past   *26*
usually   vama uku-

V
very   kakhulu
very well   hhayi-ke   *20*

W
wait   linda
wait for   lindela
wait!   yima!   *68*
wake   vuka
walk   hamba
want   funa
wash   geza
water   amanzi
way, this   kanje   *56*
way, that   kanjalo
way, what?   kanjani?   *56, 38*
we (stressed)   thina   *21*
weather   izulu   *29*
Wednesday   uLwesithathu   *23*
week   isonto
week, this   ngalelisonto   *23*
week, next   ngesonto elizayo   *23*
week, last   ngesonto eledlule   *23*
well   kahle   *56*
well then   pho, pho-ke
well, very   hhayi-ke   *20*
what?   verb + -ni?   *9*
*what is it?   yini, kuyini?   *66*
what condition?   -njani?   *57*
what price?   malini?   *54*
what sort?   -njani?   *57*
what's wrong?   kwenzenjani?   *66*
wheelbarrow   ibhala
when?   nini?   *28*
when (conj)   uma, ngesikhathi   *44*
where? (action)   verb + -phi   *9*
where? (whereabouts)   (conc) + -phi   *11*
where, it is?   kuphi   *66*
white   -mhlophe   *57*
White person   umlungu (pl) abelungu
who?   ubani?   *31, 49*
whose?   kabani?   *51*
why?   verb + -elani?   *9*
*why is it?   kungani?   *66*
will (future)   (conc) + zo-   *24*
wind   umoya
windy, it is   kunomoya   *29*
winter   ebusika
wipe   sula
wire   ucingo
with   na-   *31*
with (by means of)   nga-   *33*
work (verb)   sebenza
work (noun)   umsebenzi
work, at, to, from   emsebenzini
write   bhala
wrong, what's?   kwenzenjani?   *66*

X
Xhosa   isiXhosa

Y
year   unyaka
year, this   ngalonyaka  *23*
year, next   ngonyaka ozayo  *23*
year, last   ngonyaka odlule  *23*
yes   yebo
yesterday   izolo

*you (object)   wena (pl) nina  *22*
your   -akho (pl) enu *50*
yourself   wena  *21*
yourselves   nina  *21*

Z
Zulu (person)   umZulu (pl) amaZulu
Zulu (language)   isiZulu
Zulu, in (the language)   ngesiZulu
Zululand, in, to, from   kwaZulu

## *[Addendum]*

Additional vocabulary found in the Second Appendix is set out below:

A
animal   isilwane   (pl) izilwane
apostrophe 's sub-class nouns only   9 App II

C
can   nga   11 App II
come   -za   12 App II

D
don't (neg. instruction)   -nga-...-i   2 App II

H
her (object)   -m-   5 App II
him (object)   -m-   5 App II

M
may   -nga-   11 App II
me (object)   -ngi-   5 App II

O
object   obj concord   5 App II
of   ka (only subclass nouns)   9 App II

P
physical ailment   3 App II
please   ake u . . . e   4 App II

R
rat   igundane   (pl) amagundane

S
's apostrophe sub-class nouns only   9 App II
song   iculo   (pl) amaculo
suffer from ailment   3 App II

T
them (object)   ba-   5 App II
tree   umuthi   (pl) imithi

U
us (object)   si-   5 App II

W
what is the matter (ailment)?   3 App II
why not?   ord. neg. + ngani   1 App II

Y
you (object)   ku   5 App II